Managing India's Security Challenges

Managing India's Security Challenges

Col (Dr) Ashish Chhibbar

Manas Publications
(We Convert Fighters into Writers)
New Delhi-110002 (INDIA)

MANAS PUBLICATIONS
(We Convert Fighters into Writers)
(Publishers, Library Suppliers, Importers & Exporters)
4402/5-A, Ansari Road (Opp. HDFC Bank)
Darya Ganj, New Delhi-110 002 (India)
Off. 23260783, 23265523, Fax: 011-23272766
E-mail: manaspublications@gmail.com
manaspublications@yahoo.com

ISBN 978-81-7049-471-3
₹ 495/-

Designed at
Manas Publications

Printed in India at
HS Offsets, Delhi
and published by Mrs Suman Lata for
Manas Publications, 4402/5-A, Ansari Road
(Opp. HDFC Bank), Darya Ganj,
New Delhi-110 002 (INDIA)

Contents

Preface

India is one of the longest continuous civilizations in the world. Owning to its peculiar geography, with the great Himalayan range to the North and the Indian Ocean, Bay of Bengal and Arabian sea to the South, East and West, the Indian civilization was able to progress and prosper for a relatively longer time in a conducive environment of peace and tranquility. In spite of being sub divided into a number of small regions and kingdoms, the entire Indian sub continent was united in a multi layered and multi colored fabric of common shared beliefs, values and culture. Deep down, all Indians were alike. The foreigner who saw wide diversity in the external color, shape, size, dress, religion, language and eating habits, could not comprehend the deep underlying connect and Indian concept of Unity in Diversity.

Wars have been an inseparable part of the Indian identity. Ancient Vedic texts and religious books like Ramayana and Mahabharata give detailed and vivid accounts of epic wars and battles including use of esoteric weapons and flying machines. Not only were significant improvements made in weapons and techniques of war fighting but considerable effort was given towards evolving of strategy and statecraft. Arthashastra by Kautilya is a shining example of Indian strategic thought and its principles are as applicable in today's world as they were applicable during the Mauryan period. The Indian soldier is world renowned for his steadfastness, hardiness, pride, courage, loyalty and ability to fight and win against insurmountable odds.

The 21st century is being heralded as the century of Asia with China and India being the dominant players. The advancements in Information technology have shrunk the world into a global village with impact on a particular region being felt and having ramifications across the globe. The concept of national security itself has undergone a paradigm shift. Earlier, emphasis was on territorial expansion and integrity, whereas, presently, economic, energy, food and water security dominate a nation's security outlook. Nation states are avoiding direct confrontation and full scale all out wars. Instead, terrorism and insurgency have taken center stage. A well coordinated and executed cyber attack has the potential to cause more damage to a nation than a weapon of mass destruction. The playing field is fast becoming level with numerous state and non state actors evolving and adapting to the fluid dynamics of 21st century warfare.

In such a fast paced geo political environment, nation states are forced to take long term strategic decisions in an environment of uncertainty and unpredictability. Most of the developed countries have radically altered their national security decision making structures in order to keep pace with the changed global scenario. Understanding the evolution of our higher decision making structure and adapting it to the changed global reality is the underlying theme of this book.

Chapter 1

Introduction

We are living in interesting times. Twenty-first century has thrown unexpected challenges at us as well as afforded opportunities which were non-existent till now. Globalisation has firmly set in and events across the globe impact each and every one of our lives. Global warming is no longer a discussion topic for armchair intellectuals but is a grim reality staring us in the face. A sizeable increasing global population is faced with magnitudinal problems of climate change, disasters, recession, human rights violations, strife and unemployment. At the same time, revolution in the fields of science and technology has ensured that we live longer, lead more productive lives and are extricably linked with each other. Nation state boundaries are getting blurred with world economy moving towards a common platform where even a miniscule tremor in one part of the globe has far reaching consequences on the rest of the global community.

The new world order is in a state of flux and yet to stabilise. There is unprecedented interconnect of people, culture, resource and religion. This gives rise to uncertainty and volatility. Asian giants—China and India—are rapidly industrializing and have transformed into global manufacturing bases. They are competing and cooperating with each other at the same time. India has transformed into a major 'soft power'. Nature of war fighting has also undergone a paradigm change. Wars have not stopped. Only the methods of waging them have changed. The global community has realized the perils of all out wars. Morally, the cost of human life has increased exponentially making full fledged wars a remote possibility. Moreover, the strategic focus of nation states has shifted from land and its territorial integrity to space, oceans and poles.

The present era is the era of cooperation and survival. A number of global and regional groups have sprung up in order to project a consolidated power base for influencing global policy and negotiating with the rest of the world. Managing a nation's aspirations and security concerns in this changing global paradigm has become a complex and multi discipline task. Strategy and decision making have evolved. Super computers and simulation software can predict and war game a host of scenarios and responses. The complexity and enormity of challenges facing us are mind boggling. This adds tremendous strain to our decision making structures, which are of pre information age era and are hierarchical, cumbersome and to some extent inefficient. In order to survive and emerge victorious in today's era, we require flexible, nimble and flat decision making structures that lay down and evolve our national vision and goals, produce quality decisions in least time and implement them in an efficient and time bound manner.

Foreign Policy, National Interests and Power

Foreign Policy

Hugh Gibson has defined foreign policy as "A well rounded, comprehensive plan, based on knowledge and experience, for conducting the business of government with the rest of the world. It is aimed at promoting and protecting the interests of the nation."[1] Since the early times, when mankind transformed from hunter gatherers to cultivators and settlers, we have evolved from primitive concept of community living to complex and integrated concept of nation states and regional unions.

Nation states are constantly interacting with one another for a host of reasons ranging from trade and economy, cultural exchange and tourism, scientific collaboration, education, medicine, health care and maintenance of favourable security environment. The revolution in information technology coupled with accessible air travel has resulted in strong linkages amongst nation states with a high degree of interdependence amongst each other.

National Interests

National interests of a nation can be described as the core values and interests of that nation which directly impact the security, territorial integrity, political freedom, livelihood, aspirations and way of life of that nation. The aim of every nation's foreign policy is to create a conducive environment favourable for promoting and achieving its national interests. In order to create a conducive environment, a nation state changes or regulates its own behaviour/actions or changes/regulates the behaviour/actions of other states or does a combination of both.

Nation states are in constant competition, interaction, negotiation and co-operation with each other trying to ensure a favourable and conducive environment for its people, industries and interests. Foreign policy in effect means deciding on certain goals and making efforts to regulate behaviour of others to achieve these goals with the help of power. The national interests and power are vital ingredients of foreign policy.

Power

Power can be described as "The ability or capacity to control others and get them to do what one wants them to do and also to see that they do not do what one does not want them to do."[2] If achieving national interest is the ultimate goal of any nation, then power is the means to achieve that goal. It goes without saying that powerful nations are able to preserve and prevail upon others in order to achieve their national interests.

Power can be classified as hard power or soft power. The military might of a nation constitutes its hard power. Being a nuclear powered state, having a strong and vibrant defence forces, having capabilities to cause damage and destruction to targets accurately at far off locations, ability to wage wars at land, sea, air and space, all constitute the nation's hard power.

Hard power invokes fear and is used as a leverage to influence or force a nation into submission.

Soft power, on the other hand invokes awe, respect, trust, confidence and well being amongst nations. While hard power generally results in a win-lose situation, soft power results in a win-win situation. Economic might, vibrant democratic institutions, high level of technological research and development advancements, secular traditions, culture, gourmet, industry, entertainment, arts and craft, sports and adventure activities, active participation in international forums, peace loving and law abiding citizens, sense of security, law and order and good governance, all constitute a nation's soft power.

Comprehensive National Security

"Security does not mean simply mutual or collective self-protection in military terms of people living in different countries. It involves, in the first place, the preservation of their respective national identities in political and territorial terms. It also involves ensuring their economic well being covering all dimensions of economic security. It means creating a long term environment for durable peace, political stability and co-operation."[3] This quote by no means is an all encompassing definition of security. "There is a tradition of 50 years among the political class and bureaucracy to regard the national security as an esoteric issue to be handled only by the ministers, top level of bureaucracy and armed forces leadership."[4] The same needs to change. We can no longer be the proverbial monkey who keeps his eyes and ears closed and thinks that all is well in the world and nothing is going to happen to him. "Without nurturing the popular national security consciousness, the government machinery alone, however efficient it may be cannot tackle the problems of Indian national security with its wide and deep ramifications."[5]

As we move towards the 21st century, new and varied global challenges confront us. The world population is exponentially increasing putting enormous strain and pressure onto our eco system. There is an enormous scarcity of water, food , shelter, fuel.... Global warming is no longer a topic for discussion by the academicians but is a growing reality. There is an urgent need to cut down on our emission of green house gases, which in turn would lead to lesser industrialization; but the same is required to fill the hungry stomachs of our teeming millions. Apart from the environmental changes, our societies are also in a state of flux and upheaval. There is wide spread migration of population from the villages to towns, from one part of the nation to another, from one country to another. This coupled with growing ideological differences and spread of Naxalism/Maoism, is posing a direct threat to our internal security. Religious fundamentalism and spread of radical and fundamentalist racism is yet another threat which is manifesting in our society.

We have slowly migrated from a national to a global economy. Thanks to our vibrant economic policies, the nation has progressed and we have been able to carve out a space for ourselves in global affairs and matters. We have a right to follow a national economic policy that brings wide based prosperity to our people and does not fill the coffers of few or create islands of prosperity in seas of despair and abject poverty. This implies that in a global forum, we have to safeguard our policies and should not be coerced into signing agreements that directly impinge on our national economic aims and objectives. We also need to safeguard the vital interests of our multi national companies in a global environment. Thus, economic security is an essential and vital pillar of our national security.

Environmental Security: Teeming global population, rapid industrialization, carbon dioxide emissions and a host of other problems have placed tremendous strain on our fragile eco system. This has led to a race between nations to secure their natural resources as well as exploit natural resources of poor, corrupt and developing nations. To compound the problem, there is greater unpredictability of global weather and climate resulting in a higher frequency of floods, droughts, extreme temperatures and weather phenomena. Traditional methods of farming which depended on seasonal and predictable climate are failing resulting in food shortages in the most populated and poor countries.

Population, by far is one of the greatest challenges facing South Asia. India, Bangladesh and Pakistan are among the world's ten most populous countries. India's current population is 1.08 billion and by 2050 it is predicted to overtake China as the world's most populous country.[6] A rising population places tremendous strain on the natural resources. Green and white revolution, increasing storage capacities, use of modern agricultural means, diversification of crop pattern, use of drought and insect resistant seeds etc.

are some of the methods which can drastically increase food grain production.

Nature has been kind in providing us with adequate fresh water. However, productive and efficient use of this valuable resource needs to be carried out to ensure that we do not enter a water stress zone in coming decades.

Food Security: The rising global population and global warming, when coupled with a poor harvest and a shift from production of food grains to bio-fuels have put stocks of major food crops, especially wheat, at record low level.[7] A number of developed countries are using food grains like corn and sugarcane to produce bio fuels, especially ethanol. In 2006-07, more than 20% of the corn crop was used for ethanol production, which was nearly twice the amount used in 2002-03. This large scale conversion of crops into alternate energy source implies that the global quantity of surplus crop has drastically reduced. In the eventuality of crop failure and inadequate storage capacity, a situation can arise that in spite of having money, procurement of food grains during emergency might be increasingly difficult.

Inability to increase food production commensurate to rising population results in spiralling food costs which, in turn, gives rise to a host of inter-linked problems.

Energy Security: The Indian economy is on a roll and is predicted to be the third largest economy in the world by 2040.[8] Closely linked with the economic and development indices of any nation is the growing requirement of its energy needs. In fact, the energy requirements of a nation are more or less directly proportional to the level of industrialization and growth of that nation. This, in turn directly impacts on the global geopolitical situation as countries fiercely compete to get their share of the pie from a fast depleting reservoir of the world's energy resources, predominantly oil.

India is an energy deficit country. 30% of our import is fossil fuel and that too at a time when our energy consumption is a quarter of the developed countries consumption and is likely to increase manifold. Furthermore, coal is used as the dominant commercial fuel in India. A number of finds in the Krishna-Godavari basin and Barmer region have increased our domestic production of fuel however, it is inadequate to meet our requirements. Due to security concerns, we are finding it difficult to transport gas and oil from Iran and Central Asian countries. Development of alternate energy sources like wind, solar and nuclear are being pursued vigorously in order to reduce our dependence on fossil fuels.

Economic Security: The world has transformed itself into a global village. With rapid strides being made in the fields of telecommunications and information exchange and open system of trading with easy exchange of currency and goods, it is now possible for small and middle class traders to enter the international trading arena and sell/buy goods and services. India and China are the leading outsourcing hubs and the global economic centre of gravity is slowly shifting from west to east. Indian companies have turned multinational and are investing in emerging and developed markets. Indian goods are now accepted world wide with a reputation of providing quality at affordable prices. The impact of Indian service and BPO sector is felt world wide which have even figured in US Presidential elections as a major issue. On one hand we have made a giant transition by freeing our industry and entering the global economic arena while on the other hand we still are an agrarian economy with almost 80% of the population dependant directly or indirectly on agriculture. For us, agriculture is not a business but a way of life. Under such conditions, it is important that we play a dominant role in the global scenario and secure our economic interests. The world is slowly polarizing into cartels and groups of like-minded nations who have free trade zones amongst themselves and try to project a consolidated front at the global economic summits including WTO. ASEAN, OPEC and SAARC are examples of such associations.

References

1. Hugh Gibson, "The Road to Foreign Policy", New York, p. 9.
2. VN Khanna, "Foreign Policy of India", Vikas Publishing House Pvt Ltd, New Delhi 2012, p. 6.
3. JN Dixit, "Problems of Security in South Asia with particular reference to India", New Approach—2001 National Security, Deep Prakashan, p. 17.
4. K Subramanyam, "National Security Conscious ness", New Approach—2001 National Security, Deep Prakashan, p. 14.

5. Ibid.
6. Population Reference Bureau, 2004 World Population data Sheet p. 1. See http://www.prb.org/popin/fao/centasia/faotext1.htm. Accessed on Sept 30, 2008.
7. Poonam Munjal, "The Global Food Threat", *Business Standard*, 20 Mar 08.
8. Goldman Sachs, "Dreaming with BRICS: The path to 2050", Global economic paper, No 99, Oct 1, 2003.

Chapter 2

Indian Armed Forces and Higher Defence Organisations (Pre-Independence)

The military history of India is as old as the Indian civilization, going back several millennia. References to the rich martial traditions are contained in epics like Ramayana and Mahabharata. Geography, to a very large extent has played a major role towards shaping the extent of dynasties and evolution of military craft right through the ages. Hence, a brief on the same is a must prior to commencing our journey to explore the origin and evolution of military thought, organization, equipment and tradition in India.

Indian Sub-Continent

Geographically, the Indian sub-continent is a peninsular region in south-central Asia, rather resembling a diamond which is delineated by the Himalayas in the north, the Hindukush in the west, the Arakan in the east and which extends southward into the Indian Ocean with the Arabian Sea to the southwest and the Bay of Bengal to the southeast. Most of this region rests on the Indian Plate and is isolated from the rest of Asia by mountain barriers.

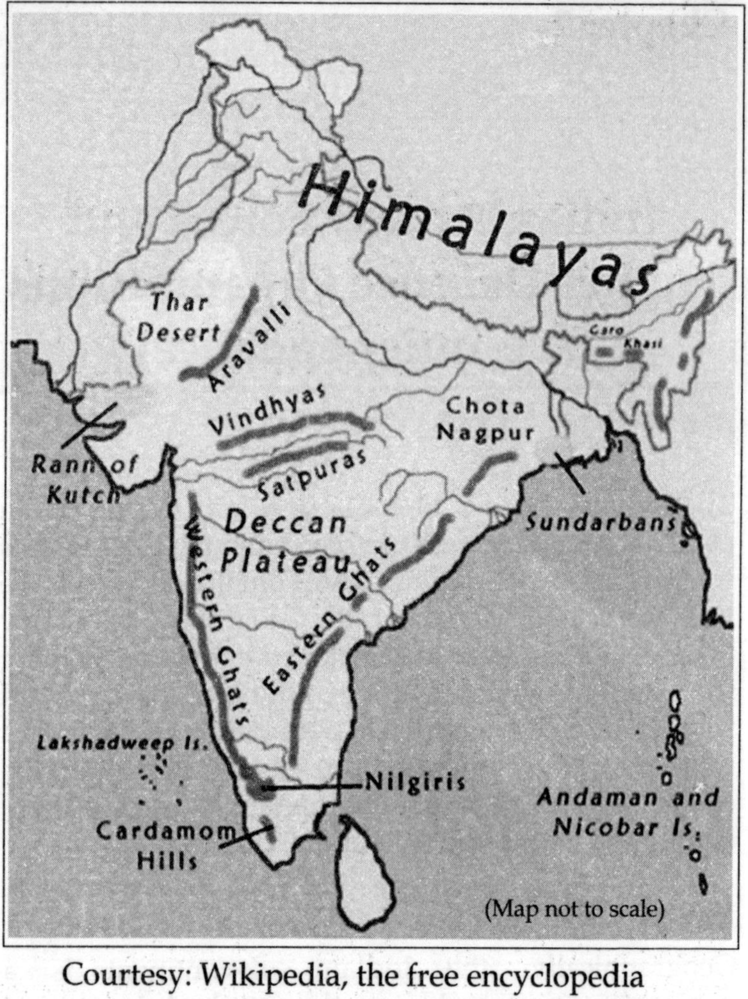

Courtesy: Wikipedia, the free encyclopedia

Thus, the Indian sub-continental land mass is covered by mountains on three sides and ocean to the south, affording it an isolated secular identity with rich resources and natural barriers conducive for civilizations to thrive for centuries without external interference.

Mountain Ranges

The Vindhya range runs across most of central India, extending approximately 1,000 kms. Geographically, it separates northern India from southern India. The western end of the range lies in eastern Gujarat, near its border with Madhya Pradesh, and runs east and north, almost meeting the Ganges at Mirzapur.

The Satpura Range begins in eastern Gujarat near the Arabian Sea coast and runs east across Maharashtra, Madhya Pradesh and Chhattisgarh. It extends 900 km. It runs parallel to the Vindhya Range, which lies to the north, and these two east-west ranges divide the Indo-Gangetic plain from the Deccan Plateau located north of river Narmada.

The Aravali Range is the oldest mountain range in India, running across Rajasthan from northeast to southwest direction, extending approximately 800 km. The northern end of the range continues as isolated hills and rocky ridges into Haryana, ending near Delhi.

The Western Ghats or Sahyadri mountains run along the western edge of India's Deccan Plateau and separate it from a narrow coastal plain along the Arabian Sea. The range runs approximately 1,600 km.

The Eastern Ghats are a discontinuous range of mountains, which have been eroded and vivisected by the four major rivers of southern India, the Godavari, Mahanadi, Krishna and Kaveri. These mountains extend from West Bengal to Orissa, Andhra Pradesh and Tamil Nadu, along the coast and parallel to the Bay of Bengal.

Highlands

The Central Highlands comprise of three main plateaus – the Malwa Plateau in the west, the Deccan Plateau in the south (covering most of the Indian peninsula) and the Chhota Nagpur Plateau in the East.

The Malwa Plateau is spread across Rajasthan, Madhya Pradesh and Gujarat. The average elevation of the Malwa plateau is 500 metres, and the landscape generally slopes towards the north. Most of the region is drained by the Chambal river and its tributaries.

The Deccan Plateau is a large triangular plateau, bounded by the Vindhyas to the north and flanked by the Eastern and Western Ghats. The Deccan covers a total area of 1.9 million square km. It is mostly flat, with elevations ranging from 1,000 to 2,000 ft. The plateau slopes gently from west to east and gives rise to several peninsular rivers such as Godavari, Krishna, Kaveri and Mahanadi which drain into the Bay of Bengal.

The Chhota Nagpur Plateau is situated in eastern India, covering much of Jharkhand and adjacent parts of Orissa, Bihar and Chhattisgarh. Its total area is approximately 65,000 sq. km and is made up of three smaller plateaus – the Ranchi, Hazaribagh and Kodarma plateaus.

Rivers

India has around 14,500 km of inland navigable waterways. There are twelve rivers which are classified as major rivers, with the total catchment area exceeding 25,28,000 sq. km. All major rivers of India originate from one of the three main watersheds:

(a) The Himalaya and the Karakoram ranges.

(b) Vindhya and Satpura range in central India.

(c) Sahyadri or Western Ghats in western India.

The Himalayan river networks are snow-fed and have a perennial supply throughout the year. The other two river systems are dependent on the monsoons and shrink into rivulets during the dry season. The Himalayan rivers that flow westward into present-day Pakistan are the Indus, Jhelum, Chenab, Ravi, Beas and Sutlej.

The Ganges-Brahmaputra-Meghana system has the largest catchment area of about 16,00,000 sq. km. The Ganges Basin alone has a catchment of about 11,00,000 sq. km. The Ganges originates from the Gangotri Glacier in Uttarakhand. It flows southeast, draining into the Bay of Bengal. The Yamuna and Gomti rivers also arise in the western Himalayas and join the Ganges in the plains. The Brahmaputra originates in Tibet, where it is known as the Yarlung Tsangpo river (or "Tsangpo"). It enters India in the far-eastern state of Arunachal Pradesh, then flows west through Assam. The Brahmaputra merges with the Ganges in Bangladesh, where it is known as the Jamuna river.

The Chambal, another tributary of the Ganges, via the Yamuna, originates from the Vindhya-Satpura watershed. The river flows eastward. Westward-flowing rivers from this watershed are the Narmada and Tapti, which drain into the Arabian Sea in Gujarat.

The river network that flows from east to west constitutes 10% of the total outflow.

Indo-Gangetic Plains

The Indo-Gangetic plains, also known as the Great Plains are large alluvial plains dominated by three main rivers, the Indus, Ganges and Brahmaputra. They run parallel to the Himalayas, from Jammu and Kashmir in the west to Assam in the east, and drain most of northern and eastern India. The plains encompass an area of 7,00,000 sq. kms. The major rivers in this region are the Ganges, Indus and Brahmaputra along with their main tributaries Yamuna, Chambal, Gomti, Ghaghara, Kosi, Sutlej, Ravi, Beas, Chenab and Tista.

The Indo-Gangetic belt is the world's most extensive expanse of uninterrupted alluvium formed by the deposition of silt by the numerous rivers. The plains are flat making it conducive for irrigation through canals. The area is also rich in ground water sources. The plains are one of the world's most intensely farmed areas. The main crops grown are rice and wheat, which are grown in rotation. Other important crops grown in the region include maize, sugarcane and cotton. The Indo-Gangetic plains rank among the world's most densely populated areas.

Thar Desert

The Thar desert is the world's seventh largest desert. It forms a significant portion of western India and covers an area of about 2,00,000 sq. kms. The desert continues into Pakistan as the Cholistan desert. Most of the Thar desert is situated in Rajasthan, covering 61% of its geographic area. About 10% of this region comprises sand dunes, and the remaining 90% consist of craggy rock forms, compacted salt-lake bottoms, and inter-dunal and fixed dune areas.

Coasts

The Eastern Coastal Plain is a wide stretch of land lying between the Eastern Ghats and the Bay of Bengal. It stretches from Tamil Nadu in the south to West Bengal in the east. The Mahanadi, Godavari, Kaveri and Krishna rivers drain these plains. The Western Coastal Plain is a narrow strip of land sandwiched between the Western Ghats and the Arabian Sea, ranging from 50 to 100 km in width. It extends from Gujarat in the north and extends through Maharashtra, Goa, Karnataka and Kerala. Numerous rivers and backwaters inundate the region. Mostly originating in the Western Ghats, the rivers are fast-flowing, usually perennial and empty into estuaries. Major rivers flowing into the sea are the Tapti, Narmada, Mandovi and Zuari.

Vedic Period[1]

In ancient times, India was populated by numerous tribes. Some indigenous and others who had migrated into the sub-continent. They were culturally and technically unevenly developed and there was constant warfare among them, particularly between the immigrants and the early settlers. These warfare over centuries produced tribal rituals, codes of chivalry and heroism, technological advancements and a hereditary group of warriors, the Kshatriya varna.

The Rigvedic tribes of Indo-Aryans were led by their tribal chieftain (Raja) and engaged in wars with each other and other tribes. They used weapons and horse-drawn spoke-wheeled chariots described prominently in the Rigveda. The main share from the booty obtained during cattle raids and battles went to the chief of the tribe. The warriors belonged to the Kshatriya varna.

The Vedas and other associated texts dating to the post-Rigvedic (Iron Age) Vedic period (1100-500 BC) contain the earliest written references to armies in India. The earliest known application of war elephants dates to this period; the animals are mentioned in several Vedic Sanskrit hymns. Ancient Indian thinkers produced two schools of war, diplomacy and interstate relations; the dharma-yuddha (ethical warfare) school; and the kuta-yuddha (devious warfare) school. The two schools were, however, not mutually exclusive. The practitioners of each school were informed by the principles and methods of the other and practised them. The best example of this is the great Mahabharata war in which one can see both schools of thought in operation. The two great epics of India, the Ramayana and the Mahabharata, refer to military formations, theories of warfare and esoteric weaponry. They discuss standing armies and the use of chariots, war elephants and even flying machines in wars.

Maurya Dynasty (265 BC)[2]

According to Megasthenes, who served as an ambassador from the Seleucid Empire, Chandragupta Maurya built an army consisting of 30,000 cavalry, 9,000 war elephants and 6,00,000 infantry. Chandragupta conquered all of northern India, establishing an empire from the Arabian Sea to the Bay of Bengal. He thereafter defeated the Macedonians and Seleucus

Nicator to conquer the regions to the east of the Indus river. He then turned south, taking over much of what is now Central India. His military was administered by six chairs, one for each of the four arms of the army (infantry, cavalry, elephants and chariots), one chair for the navy and one for logistics and supply.

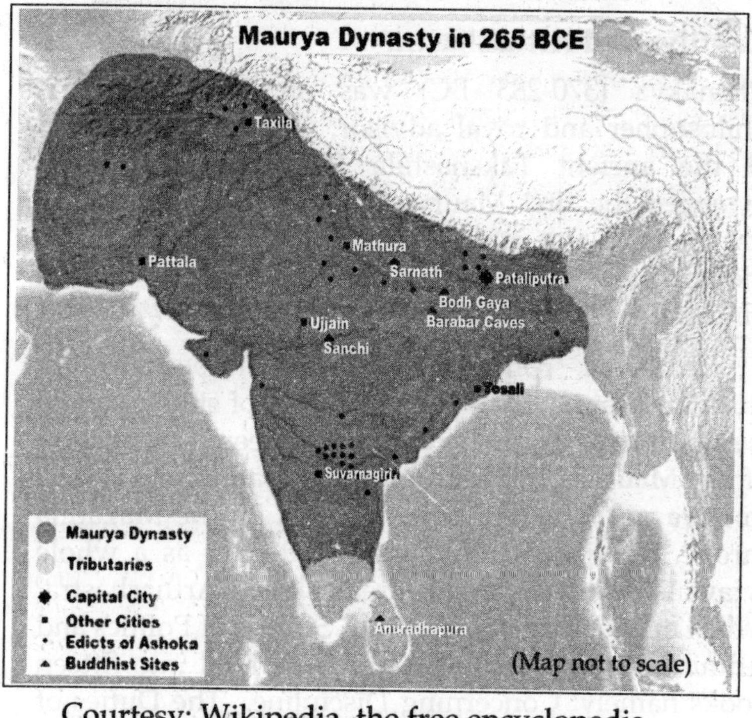

Courtesy: Wikipedia, the free encyclopedia

Infantry at this time was most commonly armed with a longbow made of bamboo and a single or double-handed broad sword probably similar to the khanda. Other foot soldiers could be armed with a large animal hide tower shield and a spear or javelins. Cavalry carried spears. Elephants were mounted, usually bareback (rarely with a howdah at this time, as it is a Greek invention), by archers or javelin throwers, with a mahout around the animal's neck. Chariots by this time were in definite decline, but remained in the army due to their prestige. In 185 BC, the last Mauryan ruler was assassinated by Pushyamitra Sunga, the Commander-in-Chief of the Mauryan armed forces.

Kautilya and Arthashastra

Chanakya (370-283 BC) was an Indian teacher, philosopher and royal advisor. Originally a teacher at the ancient Takshashila University, Chanakya managed the first Maurya emperor Chandragupta's rise to power at a young age. Chanakya served as the chief advisor to both Chandragupta and his son Bindusara.

Chanakya conceptualised the importance of studying war as an important aspect of statecraft and is said to have single-handedly engineered the victory of the Mauryas by destroying the Nanda power and to have put Chandragupta Maurya on the Magadha throne. Kautilya's thinking on statecraft as a whole is available to us in the great classic Arthashastra[3] which may be translated as the "Science of Politics and Administration". Arthashastra is divided into fifteen books namely: Concerning Discipline, The Duties of Government Superintendents, Concerning Law, The Removal of Thorns, The Conduct of Courtiers, The Source of Sovereign States, The End of the Six-Fold Policy, The Work of an Invader, Relating to War, Concerning a Powerful Enemy, Strategic Means to Capture a Fortress, Secret Means and The Plan of a Treatise.

Kautilya laid great emphasis on building forts. Defensive fortifications are required to be built on all the four corners of the kingdom. Fortifications based on mountains and water bodies are best suited to defend population centres. Forts are to be constructed using ditches, parapets, defensive fighting positions, towers, doors, pathways, chambers, obstacle systems and secret passage ways. A great deal of emphasis has been laid on the types of roads to be constructed within the fort and location of inhabitants of various castes, temples, cremation and burial grounds. The forts were supposed to be self-contained for food, water, weapons, armour and stones to withstand long hours of isolation. The forts were to be guarded by elephants, cavalry, chariots and infantry.

The Arthashastra lays down in great detail the procedure for levying of taxes, maintenance of accounts, duties of various officials, system of rewards, punishments and levying fines. A lot of emphasis was laid on inculcating spies. All aspects of public and private life were observed and reported through a vast network of spies. Spies were kept in liquor shops to see whether the expenditure incurred by customers in the shop was ordinary or extraordinary. Spies were considered to be the first line of defence by detecting strangers and misguided youth. The Arthashastra prescribes a detailed hierarchy of officers. The Senapati or Chief-of-Staff is the highest officer, his station is at the rear. Each arm i.e. Elephant, chariot, horses and infantry have their own chief. The lower commanders (nayakas) actually lead the troops in battle. The chiefs would be thoroughly familiar with the nature of war fighting in various types of terrain and climate, during day and night and conduct of different types of attacks including feint attacks. On the other hand, the Commander- in- Chief would be well versed in all kinds of weapons and in leading elephants, chariots, horses and infantry. He would be well versed in strategic planning of war including deciding the ground and time of waging war, mind of the enemy commander, strength and weakness of the enemy, how to break an enemy advance, scatter his troops, assail a fortress, when to make an advance and call a retreat.

Arthashastra lays great emphasis on policy and statecraft. Friends, enemies, mediatory and neutral types of kings have been described in great detail. Peace, war, neutrality, advance, alliance and making peace with one while waging war with another are the six forms of state policy described in Arthashastra.

Kautilya states that the knowledge of power, place, time, strength and weaknesses of own and the enemy must be known prior to launching an invasion. A detailed account is given on the layout of military camp, speed of march, distances required to be covered in a day and crossing of rivers, mountains and deserts during an advance. A strong king with overwhelming numerical superiority must only undertake an open fight. In all other circumstances, devious warfare is preferred over open fight. Devious warfare should be undertaken by striking the enemy when he is weak or in an unfavourable position. An intelligent king would create false impressions of his strength and strike at opportune moment. When an enemy's army is compact, it should be scattered. One should strike the enemy simultaneously in its front and rear. Fight the enemy with traitors and wild tribes, constantly misleading and confusing him. One should harass the enemy at night and attack him during day when his army is tired and sleepy.

The Arthashastra, goes into great detail about the "conventional" warfare of its time. Various battle formations and arrays have been described. Distances between soldiers, chariots, elephants and archers have been specified. Arthashastra dictates that one-third of the best infantry, cavalry and elephants should be kept in front and two-third on both the flanks and wings.

Arthashastra firmly believes in the strategic impact of psychological warfare against the enemy. It states that prior to launching an attack, it should infuse enthusiastic spirit amongst its ranks while at the same time portray to the enemy that it possesses super natural powers and is in close association with the gods.

The Arthashastra lays down that after capture of an enemy territory, the king should cover the enemy's vices with his own virtues by strictly observing his duties, bestowing rewards, remitting taxes and bestowing honour to the captured populace. He should adopt the life style of the people and respect their faith in order to win over their trust and confidence.

Kautilya states in Arthashastra that the arrow shot by an archer may or may not kill a single man; but skilful intrigue devised by wise men can kill even those who are in womb.

Gupta Period[4]

The Gupta Empire was an ancient Indian empire which existed from approximately 320 to 550 CE and covered much of the Indian sub-continent. Founded by Maharaja Srigupta, the dynasty is a model of a classical civilization. The peace and prosperity created under the leadership of the Guptas enabled the pursuit of scientific and artistic endeavours.

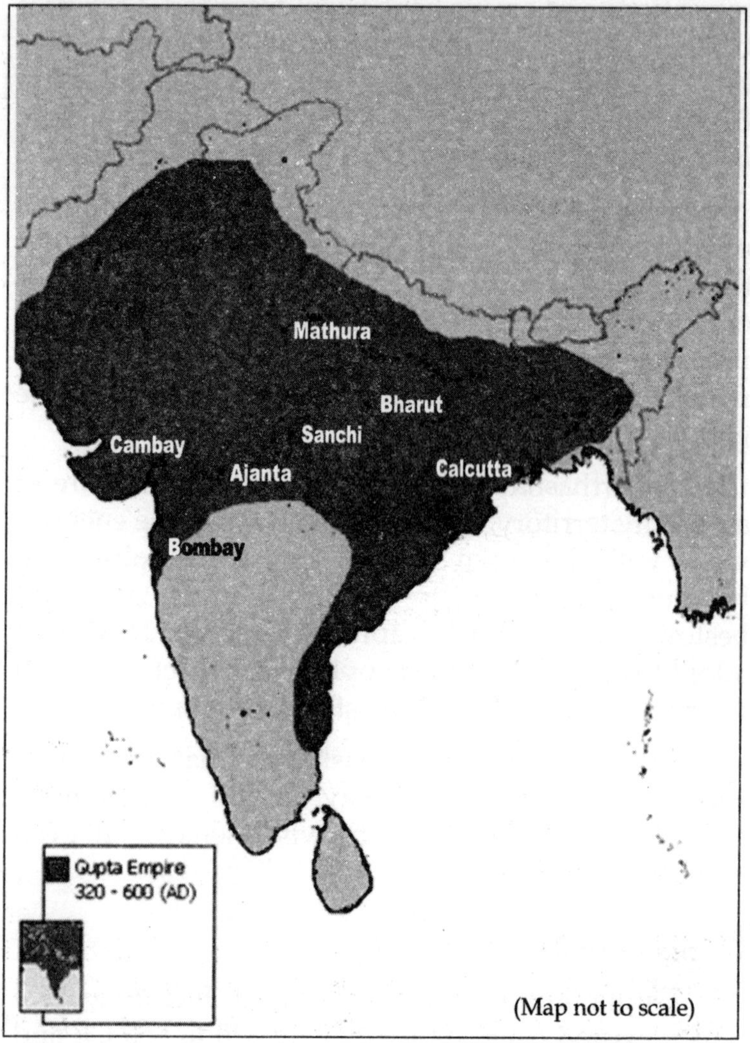

Courtesy: Wikipedia, the free encyclopedia

This period is called the Golden Age of India and was marked by extensive inventions and discoveries in science, technology, engineering, art, dialectic, literature, logic, mathematics, astronomy, religion and philosophy that crystallized the elements of what is generally known as Hindu culture. Chandragupta I, Samudragupta the Great and Chandragupta II the Great were the most notable rulers of the Gupta dynasty. The 4th century CE Sanskrit poet Kalidasa, credits Guptas with having conquered about twenty one kingdoms, both in and outside India, including the kingdoms of Parasikas (Persians), the Hunas, the Kambojas, tribes located in the west and east Oxus valleys, the Kinnaras, Kiratas etc.

The empire gradually declined because of many factors such as substantial loss of territory and imperial authority caused by their own erstwhile feudatories and the invasion by the Huna peoples from Central Asia. After the collapse of the Gupta Empire in the 6th century, India was again ruled by numerous regional kingdoms. A minor line of the Gupta clan continued to rule Magadha after the disintegration of the empire. These Guptas were ultimately ousted by Vardhana ruler Harsha Vardhana, who established an empire in the first half of the 7th century.

The Guptas seem to have relied heavily on infantry archers and the bow was one of the dominant weapons of their army. The Hindu version of the longbow was composed of metal, or more typically bamboo, and fired a long bamboo cane arrow with a metal head. Unlike the composite bows of Western and Central Asian foes, bows of this design would be less prone to warping in the damp and moist conditions often prevalent in the region. The Indian longbow was reputedly a powerful weapon capable of great range and penetration and provided an effective counter to invading horse archers. Iron shafts were used against armoured elephants and fire arrows were also part of the bowmen's arsenal. Archers were frequently protected by infantry equipped with shields, javelins and long swords.

The Guptas also had knowledge of siege craft, catapults and other sophisticated war machines. The Guptas apparently showed little predilection for using horse archers, despite the fact these warriors were a main component in the ranks of their Scythian, Parthian and Hephthalite (Huna) enemies. However, the Gupta armies were probably better disciplined. Able commanders like Samudragupta and Chandragupta II would have likely understood the need for combined armed tactics and proper logistical organization. Gupta military success likely stemmed from the concerted use of elephants, armoured cavalry and foot archers in tandem against both Hindu kingdoms and foreign armies invading from the Northwest. The Guptas also maintained a navy, allowing them to control regional waters.

During the reign of Chandragupta II, Gupta empire maintained a large army consisting of 5,00,000 infantry, 50,000 cavalry, 20,000 charioteers and 10,000 elephants along with a powerful navy with more than 1,200 ships. Chandragupta II controlled whole of the Indian sub-continent and Gupta empire was the most powerful empire in the world at that time.

Mughal Empire[5]

The Mughal Empire was the dominant power in the Indian sub-continent between the mid-16th century and the early 18th century. The Mughal dynasty was founded when Babur, hailing from Ferghana (modern Uzbekistan), invaded parts of northern India and defeated Ibrahim Shah Lodhi, the ruler of Delhi, at the First Battle of Panipat in 1526. The Mughal emperors were Central Asian Turko-Mongols from Uzbekistan, who claimed direct descent from both Genghis Khan (through his son Chagatai Khan) and Timur. The Mughal Empire superseded the Delhi Sultanate as rulers of northern India. At the height of their power in the late 17th and early 18th centuries, they controlled much of the Indian sub-continent, extending from Bengal in the east to Kabul and Sindh in the west, Kashmir in the north to the Kaveri basin in the south. Its population at that time has been estimated as between 110 and 150 million, over a territory of more than 3.2 million square kilometres (1.2 million square miles).

The greatest part of the Mughal expansion was accomplished during the reign of Akbar (1556–1605 AD). The empire was maintained as the dominant force of the present-day Indian sub-continent for a hundred years further by his successors Jahangir, Shah Jahan and Aurangzeb.

Recruitment[6]: The soldiers of the Mughal Army were not commonly recruited by the emperor himself but rather by chiefs and other leaders, who were known as Mansabdars. The Mansabdars were ranked based on the number of men that they had raised and the ranking system became known as Mansab. The highest Mansab was in command of 7,000 men, although in rare situation some were promoted to command 8,000 or even 9,000. Princes were an exception and their

Mansab ranged from 7,000 to 50,000 and beyond. Any force of horseman raised had to be comprised equally of Mughals, Afghans and Rajputs; any infantry force was required to consist of two-thirds archers and one-third matchlockmen. For each horseman, Mughals paid Rs. 200 a year. By using this money, the man provided his own horse and armour, and paid for his own and his horse's keep. Pay was not always allowed for a whole year but often only for six, five, or four months. Pay might be either *Naqd* i.e. given in cash, or Jagir i.e. an assignment of the land revenue of a certain number of villages or of a sub-division (*parganah*).

Divisions: The armed forces of the Mughals were divided into cavalry, infantry and artillery. However, cavalry was the prominent arm and was preferred over infantry and artillery. There was no division into regiments. Single troopers enlisted under the banner of a mansabdar. Thus, by successive aggregations of mansabs, a large body of troops was gathered together. From the highest to the lowest rank, the officer or soldier looked first to his immediate leader and followed his fortunes, studying his interests rather than those of the army as a whole.

Arms and Armour: The generic name for arms and armour was *silah,* plural *adah.* Underneath the body armour was worn a *qabchal* or jacket quilted and slightly ornamented. Silken trousers and a pair of Kashmiri shawls round the waist completed the costume of a nobleman of high rank. Common soldiers wore an ample upper garment, quilted thick with cotton, coming down as far as the knee. These coats would deaden the stroke of a sabre, stop the point of an arrow, and above all kept the body cool from the direct rays of the sun. The cavalry carried a great variety of arms. Most relied on were the *kotah-yaraq,* or short arms. These short arms were divided into five classes: swords and shields, maces, battle-axes, spears and daggers. Weapons for more distant attack were the bow (*kaman*) and arrow (*tir*), the matchlock (*banduq* or *tufanq*), and the pistol. Rockets were also used, but by the artillery (*topkhanah*). Mughal bowmen were considered to be especially expert in the use of their weapons. A horseman could shoot six times before a musketeer could fire twice. Archers were called *Tir-andaz.* The normal Mughal bow was called a *kaman.* It was about 4 feet long and generally shaped in a double curve. The bow was of horn, wood, bamboo, ivory and sometimes of steel. The barrels of Akbar's matchlocks were of two lengths, 66 inches and 41 inches. They were made of rolled strips of steel with the two edges welded together.

Artillery: The Mughal artillery included a variety of cannons, rockets and mines. Extremely heavy artillery was an important part of the Mughal military, especially under its early emperors. Babur deployed guns capable of firing cannonballs weighing between 225 and 315 pounds against a 1527 siege, and had previously employed a cannon capable of firing a 540 pound stone ball. Rugged passes and water crossings were insurmountable barriers and even when they could be moved, it was a slow process requiring sixteen or twenty oxen. Mughal light artillery consisted of a variety of smaller weapons. Animal-borne swivel guns saw widespread use in several forms. Elephants carried two pieces of "elephant barrel" (*Gajnal* and *Hathnal*) artillery and two soldiers to fire them. The elephants served only to transport the weapons and their crew, however; they dismounted before firing. "Camel guns" (*Shutarnal*) and "swivel guns" *zamburak*, on the other hand, were carried on camel-back and were fired while mounted. Other light guns were mounted on wheeled carts, pulled by oxen or horses. Grenadiers and rocket-bearing soldiers were also considered part of the Mughal light artillery.

Forts played an important part in Mughal times. The important forts of that period were those at Allahabad, Kalinjar, Chunar, Rohtas, Ajmer, Gwalior, Delhi, Lahore, Ranthambore, Kandhar, Kabul, Asirgarh, Daulatabad, Aurangabad, Bijapur and Golconda.

On the whole, the Mughal army was cumbersome, ill-equipped, poorly trained and followed a non-standard pattern of recruitment and war fighting. The soldiers were loyal to the Mansabdars who recruited and maintained them. The army was full of Persian, Central Asian and Afghan soldiers of fortune, whose swords were at the service of any who chose to pay them.

British Rule in India

Major Stringer Lawrence, who formed the first military units of the East India Company in Madras in 1748, organised the British Indian army into three presidencies: Bengal, Madras and Bombay. The three presidencies formed their own armies which later on constituted the Indian Army. By 1824, the size of the combined armies of Bengal, Madras, and Bombay was about 2,00,000 and had at least 170 sepoy and 16 European regiments.[7]

The armies based in Madras, Bombay and Bengal functioned as three distinct entities. Training, discipline and professionalism were the primary requirements for Indian soldiers. In 1757, Robert Clive came up with the idea of sepoy battalions for the Bengal Presidency, which were to be armed, dressed and trained as the red coats and commanded by a nucleus of British officers. The Madras Army followed suit with six battalions in 1759 followed by the Bombay Army in 1767. Recruitment in all cases was done locally amongst single castes, from specific communities, villages and families.[8] Regular cavalry regiments were raised in 1784 of which only three survived the First Independence war of 1857. Irregular cavalry were raised based on the indigenous system of raising cavalry by rulers of Indian states called the "*silladar*" system.[9]

Higher Direction of War: The three Presidencies of Bengal, Bombay and Madras were independent of each other and controlled their own armies. By the Pitt's India Act of 1784, the East India Company's rule in India came under the control of the British government. The governing council of the company was reduced to three members and the Governor-General, a crown appointee, was authorised to veto the majority decision. However, the three armies continued to maintain their independent identity, each with its own Commander-in-Chief. Overall operational control was exercised by the Commander-in-Chief of the Bengal Army, who reported to the Governor -General. In April 1895, the Presidency Armies were unified into a single Indian Army. The Indian Army was divided into four commands, Northern, Southern, Eastern, and Western. It continued to provide armed support to the civil authorities, both in combating banditry and in case of riots and rebellion. One of the first external operations the new unified army faced was the Boxer Rebellion in China from 1899 to 1901.

A Military Department[10] under a Military Member was created by the Supreme Government of the British East India Company at Kolkata in 1776. Its main function was to coordinate and record orders, relating to the Army, issued by various Departments of the Government of the East India Company. The Military Department initially functioned as a branch of the Public Department and maintained a list of Army personnel. Two Members in the Governor General's Council were responsible for military affairs. One was the Military Member, who supervised all administrative and financial matters. The other was the Commander-in-Chief who was responsible for all operational matters. All proposals of the Commander-in-Chief to the government had to be submitted through the Military member and vice-versa. The Military Department was abolished in March 1906 and was replaced by two separate Departments; the Army Department and the Military Supply Department. In April 1909 the Military Supply Department was abolished and its functions were taken over by the Army Department. The Army Department was redesignated as the Defence Department in January 1938. The Department of Defence became the Ministry of Defence under a Cabinet Minister in August 1947.

Kitchener Reforms: Lord Kitchener of Khartoum[11] was appointed the Commander-in-Chief in 1902. He immediately embarked on a series of reforms in order to transform the role and organization of the Indian Army. The principles underlying the reforms were:

- Defence of the North-West Frontier against foreign aggression was the army's primary role.
- All units were to have training and experience in that role on that frontier.
- The army's organisation should be the same in peace as in war
- Maintaining internal security was for the army a secondary role, in support of the police.

Lord Kitchener found the army scattered across the country in stations at brigade or regimental strength and providing garrisons for most of the major cities. The reformed Indian Army was to be stationed in operational formations and concentrated in the north of the sub-continent. The Commander-in-Chief's plan called for nine fighting divisions grouped in two corps commands on the main axes through the North-West Frontier. Five divisions were to be grouped on the Lucknow-Peshawar-Khyber axis, and four divisions on the Bombay-Mhow-Quetta axis. However, the cost of abandoning some thirty-four stations and building new ones in the proposed corps areas was considered prohibitive, and that aspect of the plan had to be modified.

Under the compromise adopted in 1905, the four existing commands were reduced to three, and together with Army Headquarters, arranged in ten standing divisions and four independent brigades:

- Northern Command comprised the 1st Division (Peshawar), the 2nd Division (Rawalpindi), the 3rd Division (Lahore), the Kohat Brigade, the Bannu Brigade and the Derajat Brigade.
- Western Command comprised the 4th Division (Quetta), the 5th Division (Mhow), the 6th Division (Poona) and the Aden Brigade, located in Aden in the Arabian Peninsula.
- Eastern Command comprised the 7th Division (Meerut) and the 8th Division (Lucknow).

Army Headquarters retained the 9th Division (Secunderabad) and the Burma Division under its direct control. The numbered divisions were organised so that on mobilisation they could deploy a complete infantry division, a cavalry brigade and a number of troops for internal security or local frontier defence. Permanent divisional commands were formed with an establishment of staff officers under a Major-General.

After the reforms ended in 1909, the Indian Army was organised along British lines. An Indian Army division consisted of three brigades each of four battalions. Three of these battalions were of the Indian Army and one British. The Indian battalions were often segregated, with companies of different tribes, castes or religions. One and a half million volunteers came forward from the estimated population of 315 million in the Indian sub-continent.

Regimental battalions were not permanently allocated to particular divisions or brigades, but instead spent some years in one formation and were then posted to another elsewhere. This rotating arrangement was intended both to provide all units with experience of active service on the Frontier and to prevent them becoming "localised" in static regimental stations. In contrast, the divisional locations remained constant, as indicated by their respective titles.

Lord Curzon-Kitchener Controversy: Kitchener was highly critical about the functioning of the existing Higher Defence Organisation and wanted a rational system where the advice on military matters came from only one source, but Lord Curzon who was the Viceroy was in favour of the existing system of dual advice from the Military Member as well as the Commander-in-Chief. The issue was decided in favour of Kitchener. The post of Military Member was abolished and the Military Department was redesignated as the Army Department and the Secretary came under the Commander-in-Chief. Lord Curzon resigned in protest.

During the British reign, the civil servants in Defence Department under the Defence Secretary functioned like one of C-in-C's Principal Staff Officers. Proposals by Service Headquarters went to Military Finance and when cleared, were passed to Defence Department for issuing necessary Government instructions. The proposal from Service Headquarters, which had the approval of the Chief, could not be subjected to scrutiny by the civil servants in Defence Department, as it would have meant their trying to sit in judgment over the recommendation of their own superior.

References

1. http://en.wikipedia.org/wiki/Military_history_of_India. Military history of India. Accessed on 08 May 12.
2. Ibid.
3. "Kautilya's Arthashastra", Translated into English by R Shamasastry.
4. https://en.wikipedia.org/wiki/Gupta_period. Accessed on 11 Aug 13.
5. https://en.wikipedia.org/wiki/Mughal_Empire. Accessed on 11 Aug 13.
6. https://en.wikipedia.org/wiki/Mughal_army. Accessed on 08 Aug 13.
7. https://en.wikipedia.org/wiki/Presidency_armies. Accessed on 09 Aug 13.
8. Jackson, Major Donovan (1940). India's Army. London: Low, Marston, pp. 1-8.
9. In the "silladar" system, the soldier provided his own horse, weapons and such military attire as prescribed for which he received in exchange from the state a lump sum grant and maintenance grants from time to time.
10. https://en.wikipedia.org/wiki/Ministry_of_Defence_(India) 11 Aug 13
11. https://en.wikipedia.org/wiki/Horatio_Kitchener,_1st_Earl_Kitchener

Chapter 3

Indian Armed Forces and Higher Defence Organisations (Post-Independence)

15 August 1947, not only resulted in the Independence of India but also in the creation of a new country Pakistan and widespread migration of population from either side of the border. Lord Ismay, Chief of Staff of Lord Mountbatten, was given the responsibility of planning the division of Indian Army and working out the higher defence management structure of independent India. The changes recommended by him were approved by Lord Mountbatten and accepted by the Indian Cabinet in September 1947. The three Services were given three separate Chiefs and a series of committees were set-up in our defence administration. The Defence Minister was elected by the people and responsible to the Parliament. The three Services were placed at par, each under its own Chief of Staff. As per the rules laid out in the "Government of India Allocation of Business rules" and "Government of India Transaction of Business rules", the three Services HQ have been designated

as the attached offices of the Department of Defence. The then Prime Minister, Shri Jawaharlal Nehru, had stated in the Parliament on 25 March 1955, that the Government was going into the matter of integration of the Defence Ministry and Service Headquarters.

As per the constitution, the President has been vested with the supreme command of the nation's Armed Forces. Although he is the head of the defence forces, the de facto control of these forces rests with the Cabinet, which is collectively responsible to the Parliament. A number of committees work under the Cabinet.

In a Parliamentary democracy, the cabinet or part of it headed by the Prime Minister carries the responsibility for national security and takes all decisions related to important matters, affecting national security. Initially when the Republic was formed, a Defence Committee of Cabinet (DCC) was set-up for higher direction of defence. The DCC was converted into an Emergency Committee of the Cabinet after the 1962 war and when the national emergency was lifted in 1967, this Committee gave way to Cabinet Committee of Political Affairs (CCPA).

Cabinet Committee on Security (CCS)

The Cabinet Committee on Security (CCS) is the highest policy and decision making body on national security. It is a compact body headed by the Prime Minister and its members include the Defence Minister, Home Minister, Finance Minister and Minister for External Affairs. Papers for considerations by the CCS are put up by the Ministry of Defence with the comments by other concerned Ministries. CCS can overrule any bureaucratic or military proposal.

National Security Council (NSC)

The National Security Council (NSC), along with the National Security Adviser (NSA), works parallel to the CCS. It was established on 19 November 1998, with Brajesh Mishra as the first National Security Adviser. Prior to the formation of the NSC, these activities were overseen by the Principal Secretary to the Prime Minister.

The NSC is headed by the Prime Minister and comprises of a Strategic Policy Group (SPG), a National Security Advisory Board (NSAB) and a Secretariat whose nucleus is provided by the existing Joint Intelligence Committee (JIC).

Strategic Policy Group

The Strategic Policy Group is the first level of the three tier structure of the National Security Council. It forms the nucleus of the decision-making apparatus of the NSC. This group consists of the following members:

- Cabinet Secretary
- Chiefs of Staff of the Indian Army, Navy and Air Force
- CBDT Chairman
- Director of Intelligence Bureau
- Foreign Secretary
- Home Secretary
- Defence Secretary
- Secretary (Defence Production)

- Finance Secretary
- Secretary (Revenue)
- Governor of the Reserve Bank of India (RBI)
- Secretary (Research) (i.e. head of the Research and Analysis Wing)
- Secretary of the Department of Atomic Energy
- Scientific Advisor to the Defence Minister
- Secretary of the Department of Space
- Chairman of the Joint Intelligence Committee (JIC).

The Strategic Policy Group undertakes the "Strategic Defence Review", a blueprint of short and long term security threats, as well as possible policy options on a priority basis.

Joint Intelligence Committee (JIC)

The Joint Intelligence Committee (JIC) of the Government of India analyses intelligence data from the Intelligence Bureau, Research and Analysis Wing and the Directorates of Military, Naval and Air Intelligence. The JIC has its own Secretariat that works under the Cabinet Secretariat.

National Security Advisory Board (NSAB)

The National Security Advisory Board consists of persons of eminence outside the Government with expertise in external security, strategic analysis, foreign affairs, defence, the armed forces, internal security, science and technology and economics. The board meets at least once a month and more frequently as required. It provides a long-term prognosis and analysis to the NSC and recommends solutions and address policy issues referred to it. The higher defence organization of India can be represented as under:

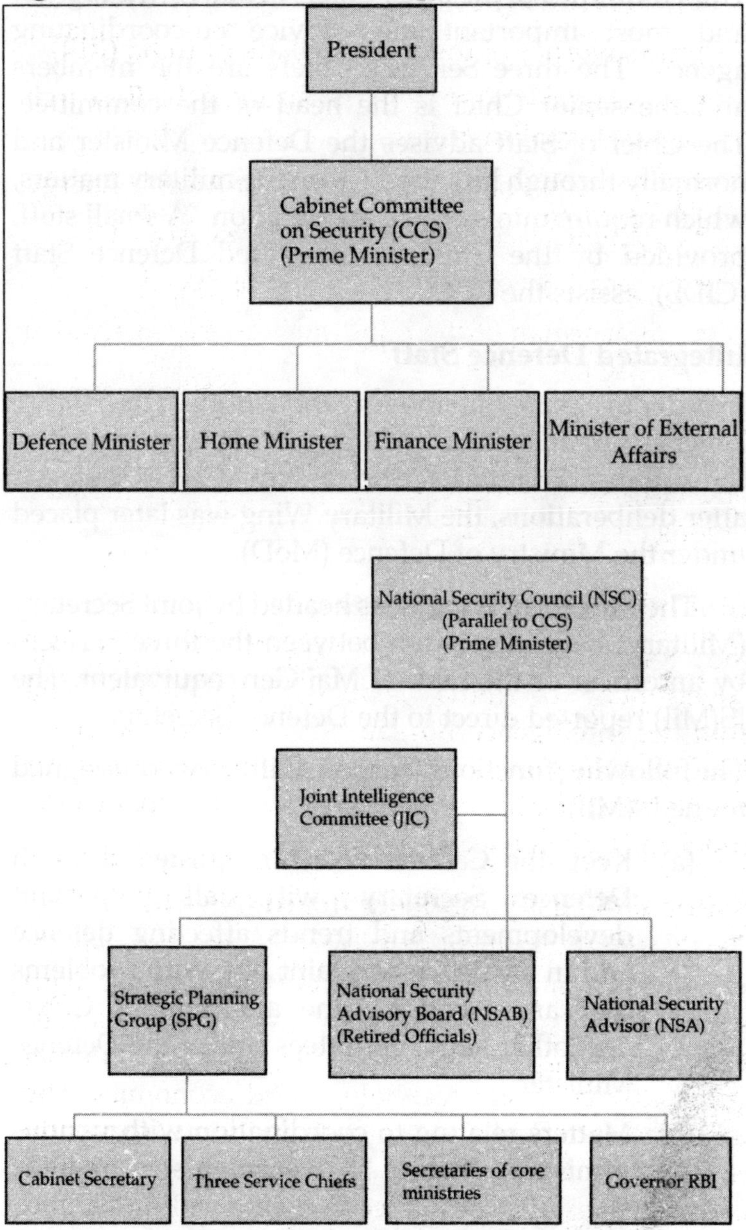

Chiefs of Staff Committee (COSC)

This committee of the three Chiefs of Staff is the highest and most important inter-service co-coordinating agency. The three Services Chiefs are the members and the senior Chief is the head of the committee. The Chief of Staff advises the Defence Minister and normally through him the CCS on the military matters, which require ministerial consideration. A small staff, provided by the Chief of Integrated Defence Staff (CIDS), assists the COSC.

Integrated Defence Staff[1]

In order to ensure the smooth functioning of the Higher Defence Organisation, a Military Wing was created in the Cabinet Secretariat from 1 Nov 1947. However, after deliberations, the Military Wing was later placed under the Ministry of Defence (MoD).

The MoD (Mil Wing) was headed by Joint Secretary (Military) held in rotation between the three Services by an officer of the rank of Maj Gen/equivalent. The JS(Mil) reported direct to the Defence Secretary.

The following functions/responsibilities were assigned to the JS(Mil):

(a) Keep the Cabinet Secretary posted through Defence Secretary with all important developments and trends affecting defence and in particular acquaint him with problems that are exercising the attention of COSC and other sub-committees under the Defence Minister.

(b) Matters relating to coordination with various Ministries/State Governments, review, amendments, publication and progress action on the Union War Book.

(c) Provide a properly constituted military machinery in the Ministry of Defence which would be in a position to interpret various details relating to defence strategy in the event of outbreak of hostilities.

(d) Process and prepare briefs on all papers relating to defence requiring CCS approval.

(e) Provide a necessary and useful link between the Defence Ministry and COSC in regard to higher defence problems.

(f) Discussions and writing of papers on all aspects of joint operational planning and close coordination with the JPC.

(g) Responsible for establishing and functioning of the Joint Services Briefing Room (JSBR)/ Control Room in erstwhile War Room Complex in South Block.

(h) To coordinate the communications/electronics requirement of the three services to include standardisation of qualitative requirements of telecommunication equipment, allocation of common user equipment, prepare joint signal plans and to render technical advice on military communications and electronics when required by three Services/MoD and prepare position papers on communication/ electronic issues.

(i) Organisation, coordination and conduct of Combined Commanders Conference, under the directions of the COSC.

(j) Within the framework of the spectrum policy and allocation of frequencies/frequency spectrum made by the National Regulatory Authority, and subject to such order of the Government thereon, to coordinate and allocate the frequency requirements of the Services in consultation, where necessary, with National Regulatory Authority.

(k) Provide the Secretariat for the following:

   (i) Defence Committee of Cabinet, since replaced by CCS.
   (ii) Defence Ministers Committee.
   (iii) Chiefs of Staff Committee (COSC)
   (iv) War Book Committee.
   (v) War Book Executive Committee.
   (vi) Principal Personnel Officers Committee.
   (vii) Principal Supply Officers Committee.
   (viii) Defence Minister's Production and Supply Committee.
   (ix) Joint Planning Committee.
   (x) Joint Training Committee.
   (xi) Joint Sea Air Warfare Committee.
   (xii) Joint Administrative Planning Committee.
   (xiii) Inter-Service Equipment Policy Committee.
   (xiv) Principal Maintenance Officers Committee.
   (xv) Joint Communication Electronics Committee.
   (xvi) Joint Electronics Warfare Board.

The organization of the JS(Mil) was merged into the Integrated Staff on formation of Headquarters Integrated Defence Staff.

Defence Planning Staff (DPS)[2]

A high level inter-service Defence Planning Staff (DPS) under the Ministry of Defence was created in 1986 to assist the COSC. It had senior inter-service staff along with senior representatives from the Ministry of Defence, Defence (Finance), Ministry of External Affairs and a senior scientist from the DRDO.

Composition: The DPS was headed by Director General Defence Planning Staff (DG DPS) held in rotation between the three services by an officer of the rank of Lt Gen/equivalent. The DPS was composed of the following divisions:

(a) International Security Division

(b) Weapons and Equipment Division

(c) Military Plans Division

(d) Policy Planning Division

Functions: The DPS was made responsible for preparation of coordinated perspective defence plans based on projections received from the Perspective Planning Directorates in the Service Headquarters, Department of Defence Production and Supplies and the DRDO. The DPS was to undertake periodic threat assessment to evolve a mix of force levels and weaponry to integrate the requirements of the three services to meet the threat. The DPS was also to undertake studies on the regions of our military interests to ensure that defence plans were oriented towards threats which the country would face during the next decade and to ensure integrated capability to meet the threats optimally within the resources available to the country. The organization of the DG DPS was merged into the Integrated Staff on formation of Headquarters Integrated Defence Staff.

Ministry of Defence (MoD)[3]

The Government of India is responsible for ensuring the defence of India and every part thereof. The Supreme Command of the Armed Forces vests in the President. The responsibility for national defence rests with the Cabinet. This is discharged through the Ministry of Defence, which provides the policy framework and wherewithal to the Armed Forces to discharge their responsibilities in the context of the defence of the country. The Raksha Mantri (Defence Minister) is the head of the Ministry of Defence. The principal task of the Defence Ministry is to obtain policy directions of the Government on all defence and security related matters and communicate them for implementation to the Services Headquarters, Inter-Services Organisations, Production Establishments and Research and Development Organisations. It is also required to ensure effective implementation of the government's policy directions and the execution of approved programmes within the allocated resources. Ministry of Defence comprises of four departments viz. Department of Defence (DoD), Department of Defence Production (DDP), Department of Defence Research and Development (DDR&D) and Department of Ex-Servicemen Welfare and also Finance Division.

Departments: The Defence Secretary functions as head of the Department of Defence and is additionally responsible for coordinating the activities of the four Departments in the Ministry. The principal functions of all the Departments are as follows:

(a) **Department of Defence:** It deals with the Integrated Defence Staff (IDS) and three Services and various Inter-Service Organisations. It is also responsible for the defence budget, establishment matters, defence policy, matters relating to Parliament, defence co-operation with foreign countries and co-ordination of all activities.

(b) **Department of Defence Production:** It is headed by a secretary and deals with matters pertaining to defence production, indigenization of imported stores, equipment and spares, planning and control of departmental production units of the Ordnance Factory Board and for Defence Public Sector Undertakings (DPSUs).

(c) **Department of Defence Research and Development:** It is headed by a Secretary, who is also the Scientific Adviser to the Raksha Mantri. Its function is to advise the Government on scientific aspects of military equipment and logistics and the formulation of research, design and development plans for equipment used by the Services.

(d) **Department of Ex-Servicemen Welfare:** It is headed by an Additional Secretary and deals with all re-settlement, welfare and pensionary matters of Ex-Servicemen.

The Finance Division of the Ministry of Defence is headed by Secretary Defence (Finance). He exercises financial control over proposals involving expenditure from the defence budget and is responsible for internal audit and accounting of defence expenditure. In the latter tasks, he is assisted by the Controller General of Defence Accounts (CGDA).

Indian Intelligence Agencies[4]

National Technical Research Organisation (NTRO): The NTRO is a premier apex scientific agency under the National Security Adviser in the Prime Minister's Office. It was set-up in 2004 and is a highly specialised technical intelligence gathering agency which acts as a super-feeder agency for providing technical intelligence to other agencies on internal and external security. The agency develops technology capabilities in aviation and remote sensing, data gathering and processing, cyber security, cryptology systems, strategic hardware and software development and strategic monitoring.

Research and Analysis Wing (RAW or R&AW): R&AW was formed in September 1968 under the helmsmanship of its first Director, Rameshwar Nath Kao. The primary function of R&AW is collection of external intelligence and counter-terrorism. In addition, it is responsible for obtaining and analysing information about foreign governments, corporations and persons to advise Indian policy-makers. It is also involved in the security of India's nuclear programme.

Intelligence Bureau (IB): The IB is India's internal intelligence agency and reputedly the world's oldest intelligence agency. Shrouded in secrecy, the IB is used to garner intelligence from within India and also execute counter-intelligence and counter-terrorism tasks.

Defence Intelligence Agency (DIA): The DIA was established on 5 March 2002 with the appointment of Lt Gen. Kamal Davar as the first Director General

(DG). It is supposed to be the nodal agency for all defence related intelligence, thus distinguishing it from the R&AW. Much of the agency's budget and operations are classified.

Higher Defence Organisation of China[5]

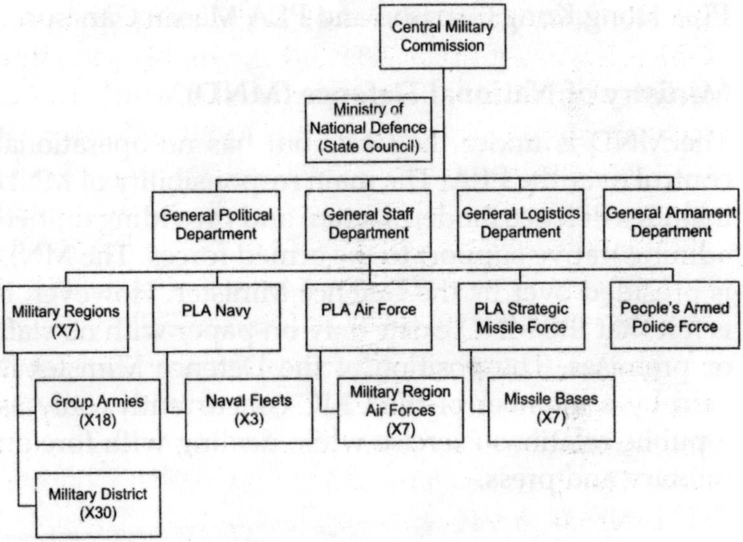

Courtesy: http://www.sinodefence.com

The Central Military Commission (CMC)

It is the apex decision making body which directly controls the People's Liberation Army (PLA), the People's Armed Police (PAP) and the reservist. The CMC is headed by a Chairman who is responsible to the Chinese Communist Party (CCP). The Chairman CMC is elected during the CCP congress, held every five years. The CMC has two or three Vice-Chairmen, who are uniformed officers under the Chairman. The composition of the CMC members keeps on varying. The members normally include the heads of the four General Departments of PLA along with the commanders of Navy, Air Force and Second Artillery Corps. Additionally, the CMC directly manages the National Defence University, Academy of Military Science, National University of Defense Technology, PLA Hong Kong Garrison and PLA Macau Garrison.

Ministry of National Defence (MND)

The MND is under the CMC but has no operational control over the PLA. The main responsibility of MND includes defence modernization and providing unified administrative support to the armed forces. The MND is presided over by the Defence Minister. However, it is felt that the MND exists only on paper with no staff or premises. The position of the Defence Minister is held by a member of the CMC concurrently, only as a public relations exercise while dealing with foreign military and press.

General Political Department

The CCP has an absolute control over the entire PLA through a complex political system. The three elements of the political system are the Party Organ system, Political officers and the Political Department.

Party Organ System: It runs parallel to the chain of command at all levels in the PLA. The Party Organ is responsible to oversee all activities being carried out by a PLA unit/establishment including operations, administration, logistics and training. It follows a hierarchical system and reports to its superior Party Organ, placed at par with the next level of PLA organization structure. At the Platoon level

'Party Cells' having three members are established. A 'Party Branch' is established at the Company level and a 'Grass root Party Committee' is established at a Battalion level. A 'Party Committee' is established at all levels of a Regiment or above.

Political Officers: The Political Officers are assigned to PLA units at every level in the Chain of Command, from the Company level up to the General Department. At Regimental Headquarter and above, the Political Officer is known as 'Political Commissar', at the Battalion level, known as 'Political Director' and at the Company level known as 'Political Instructor'. There are no Political Officers at Platoon level. The status of the Political Officer and equivalent military commander at all levels is the same. Under this system of dual responsibility and accountability, the unit commander is responsible for military matters (operations, logistics, training etc) while the Political Officer is responsible for purely political matters (ideological training, personnel affairs, security, discipline, civil military relations etc). During operations, the Political Officer serves as the unit's Second in Command.

Political Department: The Political Department is one of the four administrative departments of every PLA unit from Regimental Headquarter and above. The primary role of the Political Department is to implement the decisions of the Party Committee and to secure the support of troops for the Party's policies through political education. At Army level and above, the Political Department is also in charge of the military judicial system.

General Staff Department (GSD)

The GSD is the military command Headquarter for the PLA. It is responsible for the war planning, operations, intelligence, recruitment, mobilisation and training. It also serves as the Headquarters of the Army and oversees the operations of Navy and Air Force. According to the China's 2006 White Paper on National Defence, "the General Staff Headquarters organises and directs the development of China's armed forces and organises and commands their military operations. Under it are departments in charge of operations, intelligence, communications, military training and arms, adjutant and force structure, mobilization, electronic counter-measures, army aviation, foreign affairs, etc. Its main functions and powers are to put forward proposals on major issues of military building and operations, organize and exercise strategic command, formulate programmes, rules and regulations for military work, and organize and direct war preparations, as well as military training and mobilisation."

General Logistics Department (GLD)

The GLD is the logistics Headquarters of the PLA and is responsible for all logistics functions including housing, pay and allowances, medical, supply and transport.

General Armament Department (GAD)

The GAD is responsible for weapon system design, development, procurement, maintenance and life cycle management of weapon systems of all the services of PLA. It directly manages the PLA's nuclear and space programmes.

Army

The total strength of the Army is approximately 1.6 million personnel. Apart from Infantry, there are seven Technical Service Arms i.e. Armour, Artillery, Air Defense, Army Aviation, Engineering, Chemical Defence and Signals. The ground forces are divided into Group Armies and Provincial Military Districts. There are a total of 18 Group Armies, having regular troops numbcring from 45,000 to 60,000. Each of the PLA's seven Military Regions is assigned two to three Group Armies. The balance regular forces come under the control of the 30 Provincial Military Districts which are tasked with border defence and internal security etc. The PLA follows a hierarchical set-up from Platoon, Company, Battalion, Regiment, Division, Corps, Group Army and Military Region.

PLA Navy (PLAN)

The PLAN has a strength of approximately 2,25,000 personnel. It is divided into three fleets namely North East, East Sea and South Sea Fleets. Each fleet comprises of surface ships, submarines, naval aviation assets and coastal defence forces. The South Sea Fleet has two marine brigades. China has approximately 8 to 10 nuclear and 50 to 60 diesel electric submarines, the largest underwater capability in entire Asia.

PLA Air Force (PLAAF)

The PLAAF has transformed itself from a traditional air defence force to a multi-role force capable of undertaking limited offensive beyond Chinese borders. It operates a mixed fighter fleet consisting of J-7, J-8 II, J-10, J-11, Su-27 and Su-30 MKK multi-role aircrafts. In addition it also has in its inventory a number of support aircrafts including tankers, AEW and AWACS.

Strategic Missile Force (SMF)

The SMF is also known as the Second Artillery Corps and controls all the land based strategic as well as conventional theatre missile assets. The SMF is believed to be equipped with nuclear armed strategic missiles consisting of Dong Feng (DF) 3 and 4 series of Intermediate Range Ballistic Missile (IRBM), DF-5 Inter-Continental Ballistic Missile (ICBM) and DF-21 Medium Range Ballistic Missile (MRBM). The conventional theatre missile assets include 900 to 1,000 missiles of DF-15 and DF-11 category. In recent years the SMF has developed the DH-10 Land Attack Cruise Missile (LACM). The SMF follows a separate chain of command than regular Army and orders flow from CMC, Missile Bases, Missile Brigades and launch battalions.

Chinese Intelligence Agencies[6]

Ministry of State Security [MSS]: It is the premiere intelligence agency of China and is responsible for both internal and external intelligence gathering. The agency is divided into 12 bureaus namely First Bureau—Domestic, Second Bureau—Foreign, Third Bureau—Hong Kong, Macau and Taiwan, Fourth Bureau—Technology, Fifth Bureau—Local Intelligence, Sixth Bureau—Counter intelligence, Seventh Bureau —Circulation, Eighth Bureau—Research [Institute of Contemporary International Relations], Ninth Bureau —Anti—Defection and Counter—Surveillance, Tenth Bureau—Scientific and Technological Information,

Eleventh Bureau—Electronic Computers and Foreign Affairs Bureau

Second [Intelligence] Department: The Second [Intelligence] Department of the PLA General Staff Headquarters is responsible for collecting military information. Activities include military attaches at Chinese embassies abroad, clandestine special agents sent to foreign countries to collect military information and the analysis of information publicly published in foreign countries.

Third Department: The Third Department of the General Staff Headquarters is responsible for monitoring the telecommunications of foreign armies and producing finished intelligence based on the military information collected. The communications stations established by the Third Department of the PLA General Staff Headquarters are not subject to the jurisdiction of the provincial military district and the major military region of where they are based.

Fourth Department: The Fourth Department [ECM and Radar] of the General Staff Headquarters Department has the electronic intelligence (ELINT) portfolio within the PLA's SIGINT apparatus. This department is responsible for electronic countermeasures, requiring them to collect and maintain data bases on electronic signals.

Higher Defence Organisation of United Kingdom (UK)

In 2010, United Kingdom presented its national security strategy to the world. Titled, "A Strong Britain in an Age of Uncertainty: The National Security Strategy", the document was placed in front of the Parliament by the Prime Minister in Oct 2010. The strategy document lists counter terrorism, cyber, international military crisis and disasters as the current priority areas for the government from the security point of view. The national security policy is based on four major tenets. Firstly, emphasis on spotting emerging risks and dealing with them before they became crisis. Secondly, seamless co-operation between the military and civilian agencies in stabilising fragile states. Thirdly, having a much closer relationship between government, private sector and public and lastly, ensuring that the decisions on the future of the Armed forces receive the most attention.

National Security Council (NSC)

The National Security Council (NSC) was established on 12 May 2010 and is a Cabinet Committee tasked with overseeing all issues related to national security, intelligence coordination, and defence strategy. The NSC brings together, in a weekly meeting, the full range of national security departments alongside military and intelligence chiefs, supported by a senior permanent secretary as the Prime Minister's National Security Adviser.

Intelligence plays a vital role in the work of the National Security Council, with the heads of all three intelligence services, the National Security Adviser and the Chairman of the Joint Intelligence Committee attending its meetings. The National Security Adviser now acts as the coordinator for intelligence, responsible to the Prime Minister as Minister for the Intelligence Services. The NSC is headed by the Prime Minister. Other members include the Deputy Prime Minister,

Chancellor of the Exchequer, Secretary of State for Foreign and Commonwealth Affairs, Secretary of State for Defence, Secretary of State for the Home Department, Secretary of State for International Development and Secretary of State for Energy and Climate Change.

Ministry of Defence

The Ministry of Defence (MoD) is responsible for implementing the defence policy and is the headquarters of the British Armed Forces. The MoD also manages day-to-day running of the armed forces, contingency planning and defence procurement. The Ministers and Chiefs of the Defence Staff are supported by a number of civilian, scientific and professional military advisors. The Permanent Under-Secretary of State for Defence (generally known as the Permanent Secretary) is the senior civil servant at the MoD. His or her role is to ensure the MoD operates effectively as a department of the government. Three main committees are constituted to manage the affairs of the MoD.

Defence Board: The Defence Board is the highest committee in the Ministry of Defence (MoD). It is responsible for the full range of defence business, other than the conduct of operations. Chaired by the Secretary of State, the Defence Board is the main corporate board of the MoD, providing senior level leadership and strategic management of defence, driving forward delivery and change. The current membership of the Defence Board is: the Secretary of State; the Armed Forces Minister; the Permanent Secretary (the most senior civilian in the Department); the Chief of the Defence Staff (the professional head of the Armed Forces); the Vice Chief of the Defence Staff (the Chief Operating Officer for the Armed Forces element of defence business); the Chief of Defence Material (the head of Defence Equipment and Support); the Director General Finance; and three non-executive Board members.

Defence Council: The Defence Council is the senior departmental committee. It is chaired by the Secretary of State, and comprises the other Ministers, the Permanent Under-Secretary, the Chief of Defence Staff and senior service officers and senior officials who head the Armed Services and the department's major corporate functions. It provides the formal legal basis for the conduct of defence in the UK through a range of powers vested in it by statute and Letters Patent.

Defence Business Services (DBS): The formation of DBS brings together a range of corporate services that were previously delivered by different parts of the MoD to form one delivery organisation managed through a single top management structure.

The Ministry of Defence includes a number of organizations. These are:

(a) Central Command Organisations:

(i) Air Command
(ii) Army Headquarters
(iii) Navy Command
(iv) Joint Forces Command
(v) Head Office and Corporate Services (HOCS)

(b) Support Organizations:

(i) Defence Business Services (DBS)

(ii) Defence Equipment and Support (DE&S)

(iii) Defence Infrastructure Organisation (DIO)

(c) Executive Agencies:

(i) Defence Science and Technology Laboratory (DSTL)

(ii) Defence Support Group (DSG)

(iii) UK Hydrographic Office (UKHO)

(d) Non-Departmental Public Bodies:

(i) National Army Museum

(ii) National Museum of the Royal Navy

(iii) Royal Air Force Museum

Chief of Defence Staff (CDS)

The Chief of Defence Staff is the professional head of the British Armed Forces and the most senior uniformed military adviser to the Secretary of State for Defence and the Prime Minister. The Chief of the Defence Staff is based at the Ministry of Defence and works alongside the Permanent Under Secretary, the Ministry's senior civil servant. He is supported by the Vice Chief of Defence Staff and the professional heads of the three services i.e. First Lord and Chief of the Naval Staff, Chief of the General Staff and Chief of the Air Staff.

UK Intelligence Agencies

Secret Intelligence Service (SIS) or MI6: The SIS, often known as MI6, collects Britain's foreign intelligence and provides the Government with a global covert capability to promote and defend the national security and economic well-being. The Secret Intelligence

Service (SIS) was established in 1909 as the Foreign Section of the Secret Service Bureau.

Government Communication Headquarters (GCHQ): The GCHQ provides signal, cipher and cyber intelligence to the British Government. The GCHQ dates back its history to pre World War I era and played a crucial role during the World Wars in deciphering and intercepting many important German messages.

Security Service MI5: The Security Service, is the UK's national security intelligence agency. It is responsible for protecting the UK against threats to national security from espionage, terrorism and sabotage, from the activities of agents of foreign powers, and from actions intended to overthrow or undermine parliamentary democracy by political, industrial or violent means.

Reforms in UK Higher Defence Structure[7]

On 13 August 2010, the UK Defence Secretary launched a full and fundamental review of the defence decision making and implementation structures. A steering group, chaired by Lord Levene, drawn primarily from outside the MoD, was convened. The 2nd Permanent Secretary (2nd PUS) and Vice Chief of the Defence Staff (VCDS) sat on the steering group to provide defence expertise and a departmental perspective.

The terms of reference set out were to conduct a fundamental review of how the MoD is structured and managed, in order to design a model for departmental management which is simpler and more cost effective, with clear allocation of responsibility, authority and accountability.

Proposed Defence Reforms: The reforms committee has made the under mentioned recommendations:

(a) Strengthened Top-Level Decision-Making: It should be centred on a new and smaller Defence Board chaired by the Defence Secretary, with another Minister, the PUS, CDS, DG Finance, Chief of Defence Material and three Non-Executive Directors as members, responsible for providing strategic direction to the Department and holding it to account. The new Defence Board should be the primary decision-making body for non-operational matters. It should meet ten times a year. A formal sub-committees to the new Defence Board should be established to conduct investment approvals (Investment Approvals Committee), audit (Defence Audit Committee) and to oversee the career management system for senior civilians and military officers (Appointments Committee).

(b) Role and Responsibilities of Appointments: The Permanent Secretary and Chief of Defence Staff should continue jointly to lead Defence, but with their roles and responsibilities clarified. PUS and CDS should be jointly responsible for strategy and should chair a new 'strategy' group to support them in delivering this function. CDS should continue to convene a Chiefs of Staff Committee meeting in 'operations' mode to support him in his operational responsibilities. He should also convene a Chiefs of Staff Committee meeting in 'Armed Forces' mode to inform but not constrain his contribution on the new Defence Board.

(c) Head Office: A key role for the Head Office is to assist Ministers, PUS and CDS in setting the direction for the Department and the Armed Forces.

It supports PUS as the lead on policy advice and CDS as strategic military commander. The Government will publish a National Security Strategy (NSS) and conduct a Strategic Defence and Security Review (SDSR) each Parliament. The NSS and SDSR will be the means by which the Government determines the high level direction on the tasks the Armed Forces should undertake and plan for now and in the future.

(d) Services: The Service Chiefs should remain responsible for the overall leadership and custodianship of their Service, and should continue to provide operational advice to CDS and, when required, Ministers, on the employment of their Service. The Service Chief's 'direct' role in departmental strategy, resource allocation and defence management should be reduced, though PUS and CDS should continue to seek their advice on issues relating to their Service as appropriate. As a result of these changes to the role of the Service Chiefs, and to avoid duplication, the Services should no longer need a 4 star Commander-in-Chief, although this will also require further changes of responsibility at the 3 star level. The Service Chiefs' principal supporting staff should be based at their Service headquarters, with a much reduced staff, headed at two-star level, based in Head Office.

(e) Financial Management: It should be considerably strengthened and there should be a widely-shared culture of managing defence within available resources and realistic assumptions about the longer-term budget. At the centre, the DG Finance should be a member of the new Defence Board, chair its Investment Approvals Committee (IAC) and set standards and policy for financial management across

Defence. Responsibility and accountability should be aligned for all Top Level Budget (TLB) holders, with responsibility and budgets for detailed capability planning passing to the Service Chiefs and Commander Joint Force Command.

(f) Jointness: Some military capabilities have to be integrated on a 'joint' basis in order to effectively enable operations. To that end, a Joint Forces Command should be created to manage and deliver specific joint capabilities and to take the lead on joint warfare development, drawing on lessons and experimentation to advise on how the Armed Forces should conduct joint operations in the future. The Joint Forces Command should be led by a military 4 star, and should have responsibility for commanding and generating the joint capabilities allocated to it and setting the framework for joint enablers that sit in the single Services. As a result, a number of military organisations currently managed by the Central TLB should pass to the Joint Forces Command. The Permanent Joint Headquarters should sit within the Joint Forces Command, but report for operational purposes direct to the CDS.

(g) Operations: All military operations will be centred on the Permanent Joint Headquarters (PJHQ). In principle, and to simplify roles, the Department should look to make PJHQ responsible for all military operations and should consider whether those operations not currently run by PJHQ should be transferred to it.

(h) Enabling Services: The Enabling services should be delivered as efficiently, effectively and professionally as possible, including through the creation of the new Defence Infrastructure and Defence Business Services organisations.

(j) People: It involves development of the 'Whole Force Concept', which seeks to ensure that Defence is supported by the most cost-effective balance of regular military personnel, reservists, MoD civilians and contractors. The size of the senior cadre of Defence and the management levels below it to be reduced. To enable this, the Department should review all non-front line military posts from OF5 (Captain/Colonel/Group Captain) and civilian posts from Band B (Grade 7), to determine the need for the post, whether it needs to be civilian or military, and optimum management structures. The Department should manage and use its senior military and civilian personnel more effectively. The career management system should be designed so that individuals stay in key senior posts for longer and the processes for promotions and appointments are transparent and (on the military side) standardised, to provide assurance that both Defence and Service needs are being met.

Higher Defence Organisation of USA

National Security Council (NSC)

The White House National Security Council (NSC) is the principal forum used by the President of the United States for considering national security and foreign policy matters with his senior national security advisors and Cabinet officials and is part of the Executive Office of the President of the United States. Since its inception in 1947 under Harry S. Truman, the function of the Council has been to advise and assist the president on national security and foreign policies. The Council also serves as the president's principal arm for coordinating these policies among various government agencies.

The National Security Council is chaired by the President. Its regular attendees (both statutory and non-statutory) are the Vice-President (statutory), the Secretary of State (statutory), the Secretary of Defence (statutory), the National Security Advisor (non-statutory) and the Secretary of Treasury (non-statutory). The Chairman of the Joint Chiefs of Staff is the statutory military advisor to the Council, the Director of National Intelligence is the statutory intelligence advisor, and the Director of National Drug Control Policy is the statutory drug control policy advisor.

The Chief of Staff to the President, Counsel to the President, and the Assistant to the President for Economic Policy are also regularly invited to attend NSC meetings. The Attorney General and the Director of the Office of Management and Budget are invited to attend meetings pertaining to their responsibilities. The heads of other executive departments and agencies, as well as other senior officials, are invited to attend meetings of the NSC when appropriate. The chain of command of the US Armed forces runs from the President to the Secretary of Defence directly to the commanders of the Unified Combatant Commands. The chiefs of respective services do have authority over personnel assignments and oversight over resources and personnel allocated to the combatant commands within their respective services.

Department of Defence (DoD)

The DoD is headed by the Secretary of Defence and has three subordinate military departments: the US Department of the Army, the US Department of the Navy, and the US Department of the Air Force. In addition, there are many Defence Agencies such as the Defence Intelligence Agency (DIA), the National Security Agency (NSA), the National Geospatial-Intelligence Agency (NGA), the National Reconnaissance Office (NRO), the Defence Advanced Research Projects Agency (DARPA), the Defence Logistics Agency (DLA), the Missile Defence Agency, and the Pentagon Force Protection Agency (PFPA), all of which are under the command of the Secretary of Defence. DoD also operates several joint services schools, including the National Defence University (NDU) and the National War College (NWC).

The Department of Defence is composed of the Office of the Secretary of Defence (OSD), the Joint Chiefs of Staff (JCS) and the Joint Staff (JS), Office of the Inspector General (DoDIG), the Combatant Commands, the Military Departments [Department of the Army (DA), Department of the Navy (DON) and Department of the Air Force (DAF)], the Defence Agencies and DoD Field Activities, the National Guard Bureau (NGB).

Chairman Joint Chiefs of Staff (CJCS)

The CJCS is the highest-ranking military officer in the United States Armed Forces and is the principal military advisor to the President of the United States, the National Security Council, the Homeland Security Council and the Secretary of Defence. While the Chairman of the Joint Chiefs of Staff outranks all other officers, he does not have operational command authority over the Armed Forces.

The Chairman convenes the meetings and coordinates the efforts of the Joint Chiefs of Staff (JCS), an advisory body within the Department of Defence comprising the Chairman, the Vice-Chairman of the Joint Chiefs of Staff, the chiefs of staff of the United States Army and United States Air Force, the Chief of Naval Operations, the Commandant of the Marine Corps, and the Chief of the National Guard Bureau.

Unified Combatant Commands (UCC)

A Unified Combatant Command (UCC) is composed of forces from at least two Military Departments and has a broad and continuing mission. These commands are established to provide effective command and control of US military forces, regardless of branch of service, in peace and war. They are organized either on a geographical basis known as "Area of Responsibility", (AOR) or on a functional basis. Presently, there are nine Unified Combatant Commands of which six have regional responsibilities and three have functional responsibilities. Each unified command is led by a Combatant Commander (CCDR), who is a four-star general or admiral. CCDRs exercise combatant command (COCOM), a specific type of non-transferrable command authority over assigned forces, regardless of branch of service, that is vested only in the CCDRs by federal law. The nine combatant commands are United States Africa Command, United States Central Command, United States European Command, United States Northern Command, United States Pacific Command, United States Southern Command, United States

Special Operations Command, United States Strategic Command and United States Transportation Command.

US Intelligence Agencies[8]

The United States Intelligence Community (IC) is a federation of 16 separate United States government agencies that work separately and together to conduct intelligence activities considered necessary for the conduct of foreign relations and national security of the United States. Member organizations of the IC include intelligence agencies, military intelligence and civilian intelligence and analysis offices within federal executive departments. The IC is led by the Director of National Intelligence (DNI), who reports to the President of the United States.

Central Intelligence Agency (CIA): The CIA is an independent agency responsible for providing national security intelligence to senior US policy-makers. The CIA is separated into four basic components: the National Clandestine Service, the Directorate of Intelligence, the Directorate of Science and Technology, and the Directorate of Support. The National Clandestine Service (NCS) has responsibility for the clandestine collection of foreign intelligence, primarily human source intelligence (HUMINT). The Directorate of Intelligence (DI) analyzes all-source intelligence and produces reports, briefings and papers on key foreign intelligence issues. This information comes from a variety of sources and methods, including US personnel overseas, agent reports, satellite photography, foreign media and sophisticated sensors. The Directorate of Science and Technology (DS&T) accesses, collects and exploits information to facilitate the execution of the Agency's mission by applying innovative, scientific, engineering and technical solutions to the most critical intelligence problems. The DS&T incorporates over 50 different disciplines ranging from computer programmers and engineers to scientists and analysts. The Directorate of Support (DS) provides support that is critical to the Agency's intelligence mission. The DS delivers a full range of support, including: facilities services, financial management, medical services, logistics and the security of Agency personnel, information, facilities and technology.

Defence Intelligence Agency (DIA): The DIA is the central producer and manager of foreign military intelligence for the United States, specializing primarily in human intelligence, as well as measurement and signature intelligence. Although the DIA is designated a Department of Defence (DoD) combat support agency, the majority of its 16,500 employees (65%) are civilian and its intelligence operations in support of US national strategic planning extend far beyond the zones of combat. The agency has its own Clandestine Service, which conducts espionage activities around the world, particularly in countries where the DoD has better access or more specialized military experts than the over-extended Central Intelligence Agency (CIA).

National Security Agency (NSA): The NSA is the central producer and manager of signals intelligence for the United States. Estimated to be one of the largest of US intelligence organizations in terms of personnel and budget, the NSA operates under the jurisdiction of the Department of Defence and reports to the Director of National Intelligence. The NSA is primarily tasked with global monitoring, collection, decoding, translation and analysis of information and data for foreign intelligence and counter intelligence purposes. The NSA is also responsible for the protection of US government communications and information systems.

National Geospatial-Intelligence Agency (NGA): The NGA is a combat support agency of the United States Department of Defence with the primary mission of collecting, analyzing and distributing geospatial intelligence (GEOINT) in support of national security. NGA was formerly known as the National Imagery and Mapping Agency (NIMA). The NGA was credited by White House and military officials with providing critical information in support of Operation Neptune's Spear on May 2, 2011, in which the United States military raided a secret compound in Abbottabad, Pakistan, and killed Osama bin Laden.

National Reconnaissance Office (NRO): The NRO designs, builds, and operates the spy satellites of the United States government and provides satellite intelligence to several government agencies, particularly signals intelligence (SIGINT) to the NSA, imagery intelligence (IMINT) to the NGA and measurement and signature intelligence (MASINT) to the DIA.

Goldwater Nichols Act[9]

The Goldwater-Nichols Department of Defence Reorganization Act of 1986 reworked the command structure of the United States military. It increased the powers of the Chairman of the Joint Chiefs of Staff implementing some of the suggestions from the Packard Commission, commissioned by President

Ronald Reagan in 1985. It made the most sweeping changes to the United States Department of Defence since the department was established in the National Security Act of 1947.

Named after Senator Barry Goldwater (R-Arizona) and Representative William Flynt "Bill" Nichols (D-Alabama), the bill passed the House of Representatives, 383-27, and the Senate, 95-0. It was signed into law by President Reagan on October 1, 1986. Admiral William J. Crowe was the first Chairman to serve under this new legislation. Among other changes, Goldwater-Nichols streamlined the military chain of command, which now runs from the President through the Secretary of Defence directly to unified combat commanders, bypassing the service chiefs who were assigned an advisory role.

Chain of Command and Military Advice: Under the Goldwater-Nichols Act, military advice was centralized in the Chairman of the Joint Chiefs as opposed to the service chiefs. The Chairman was designated as the principal military adviser to the President of the United States, National Security Council and Secretary of Defence. The act also established the position of Vice-Chairman of the Joint Chiefs of Staff and simplified the chain of command. It increased the ability of the Chairman to direct overall strategy, but provided greater command authority to "unified" and "specified" field commanders. The Chairman may not exercise military command over the Joint Chiefs of Staff or any of the armed forces (section 152c of the Act).

Interaction of Services: Goldwater-Nichols changed the way the services interact. The services themselves "organize, train and equip" forces for use by the combatant commanders (COCOMs) and the service chiefs no longer exercise any operational control over their forces. Rather than reporting to a service chief operationally, the service component forces support the COCOM responsible for a specific function (Transportation, Strategic, Joint Forces, and Special Operations), or a geographic region of the globe (Europe, Middle East, etc.). The COCOM then fielded a force capable of employing Air Land Battle doctrine (or its successors) using all assets available to the military. The restructuring afforded a combination of effort, integrated planning, shared procurement and a reduction or elimination in inter-service rivalry. It also provided unity of command, conforming with leading military science. Individual services changed from relatively autonomous war-fighting entities into organizational and training units, responsible for acquisition, modernization, force-development and readiness as a component of the integrated force. Thus USCENTCOM (US Central Command) for example, would be assigned air, ground and naval assets in order to achieve its objective, not the inefficient method of individual services planning, supporting and fighting the same war.

Personnel Management of Officers: Another major effect of the Act is the way it has dramatically changed the personnel management of military officers. Officers are routinely assigned to Joint Duty positions and are educated in Department of Defence joint professional development schools as part of their career development and progression. For example, in order to be eligible for promotion to Flag Officer rank (i.e., Admirals and Generals), colonels (Army, Marine

Corps, and Air Force) or Navy captains must have had at least one Joint Duty assignment.

Shared Procurement: Shared procurement allowed the various branches to share technological advances such as stealth and smart weapons quickly and provided other ancillary benefits (such as the inter-operability of radios between services, heretofore unknown in the military). Joint implementation of new technology allowed for joint development of supporting doctrine. Therefore, the Goldwater Nichols Act could be seen as the initial step of the currently ongoing Revolution in Military Affairs (RMA) with its concept of Network Centric Warfare (NCW). Without the restructuring, i.e. integration of the three branches and improvement of underlying processes, NCW would be unthinkable. Conceptually it was tailored to Cold-War symmetric threats.

References

1. Organisation of Integrated Defence staff. From http://ids.nic.in. Viewed on 23 Jun 08.
2. Ibid.
3. Organisation of Ministry of Defence. From http://mod.nic.in. Viewed on 16 May 08.
4. Extract taken from http:://www.wikipedia.com. Accessed on 28 Aug 13.
5. https://www.sinodefence.com. Accessed on 13 Aug 13.
6. https://www.fas.org/irp/world/china/index.html. Accessed on 30 Aug 13

7. Defence Reform: An independent report into the structure and management of the Ministry of Defence", Extract from http::/ /www.mod.uk. Accessed on 10 Jan 2013.
8. Extract taken from http::/ /www.wikipedia.com. Viewed on 01 Sep 13
9. Ibid. Accessed on 21 Jun 2010.

Chapter 4

Environmental Scan: 2020 AD

Introduction

The twenty-first century is proving to be a very violent and unpredictable one. Nations have been inter-meshed with each other to a very large extent and the concept of a super power has more or less finished. The inter-dependence between different nations has increased to such an extent that no nation can now claim to be self-sufficient in all its needs. The two major drivers of change in this century have been Information Technology (IT) and Global Economy. The first has ensured the multi layered inter-meshing of nations into one entity or global village where distances and geography do not matter. The other has ensured the collective make or break phenomena wherein happenings in one nation have a collective response across the globe making decision making even more challenging. There has been a rise in non-state actors and Islamic terrorism. The century has witnessed increased levels of violence due to terrorism in South Asia and for the first time strategic terrorist attacks have been mounted against USA and Europe.

Water, food and fuel continue to be scarce as the world population spirals out of control. Unregulated world markets have resulted in a financial downfall and recession of such a magnitude so as to parallel that of the great depression of 1929. The increased interdependence has ensured that the tremors of this downfall have been witnessed by one and all. On the other hand, global warming and climate change are no longer myths but looming realities. On one hand malaria still continues to be one of the largest killers of mankind while on the other spectacular results and breakthroughs have been achieved in the fields of genetic engineering and stem cell research. On the whole, the world is witnessing change at such a fast pace which it has never witnessed before. Alvin and Heidi Toffler, futurologist have described three titanic shifts called waves in the world history which had the power to change the complete world. The first wave was the Agricultural wave. The second was the Industrial wave and third the Information wave. The time span of each wave is shrinking exponentially. The **information age** can be said to start in the seventies and is rapidly changing into the **Instant age** presently. The Instant age is putting tremendous pressures on our decision-makers. Gone is the era when decisions could be made at leisure and implemented at will. **The present age requires instant decisions, accurate decisions and instant implementation. If we falter on any one of these three counts, we are doomed to perish.**

Geopolitical Situation

The world politics in the post-Cold War period has moved apace, but with markings of uncertainty and instability. Conceptions of security and stability, and offence and defence have undergone transformations. Today's international security system is characterised by the American pre-eminence and unilateralism; continuing and increased role of nuclear weapons as means of political blackmail, conflict and deterrence; role of rapid technological developments in national security management; regional security problems; and emergence of non-state actors as a source of national and international instability.[1]

Power plays in the international arena have eroded the sanctity of the nation state. The phenomenon of the legitimized intervention is one of the major characteristics of the contemporary world. Intervention is legitimized for the protection of oppressed minority groups, prevention of environmental degradation, for securing human rights, for the preservation of democracy and to prevent excessive militarisation or irresponsible arms acquisition. The second factor which has affected the notion of territorial sovereignty is the consolidation of economy regional blocs. Increased concentration on regional alliances for the purposes of trade, commerce and tourism has rendered borders irrelevant. The shift from "geopolitics" to "geoeconomics" has meant that a much greater role is played by trading and commercial companies in transcending territorial boundaries. Thirdly, the enlarged flows of communication, information, media images, population and commodities, means that each country is increasingly integrated into the world system, on often very unfavourable terms. Indeed, studies have shown that globalization exacerbates inequality.

The international security system during the Cold War was based on bipolarity and was predictable. During this period, the world survived without major wars in a highly competitive security regime between the United States and the Soviet Union. The end of the Cold War has brought about major consequences for the international security system and hence new policy problems for various states in the developing world. Now the predictability of the Cold War has given way to uncertainty and complexity. Many of the strategic assumptions of the past have changed.

The US National Intelligence Council 2020 Project in its report "Mapping the Global Future" brings out certain key changes in the global geopolitical situation in the year 2020. It states that the likely emergence of China and India as new major global players—similar to the rise of Germany in the 19th century and the United States in the early 20th century—will transform the geopolitical landscape, with impacts potentially as dramatic as those of the previous two centuries.[2] A combination of sustained high economic growth, expanding military capabilities, active promotion of high technologies and large populations will be at the root of the expected rapid rise in economic and political power for both countries. Because of the sheer size of China's and India's populations—projected by the US Census Bureau to be 1.4 billion and almost 1.3 billion respectively by 2020—their standard of living need not approach Western levels for these countries to become important economic powers.

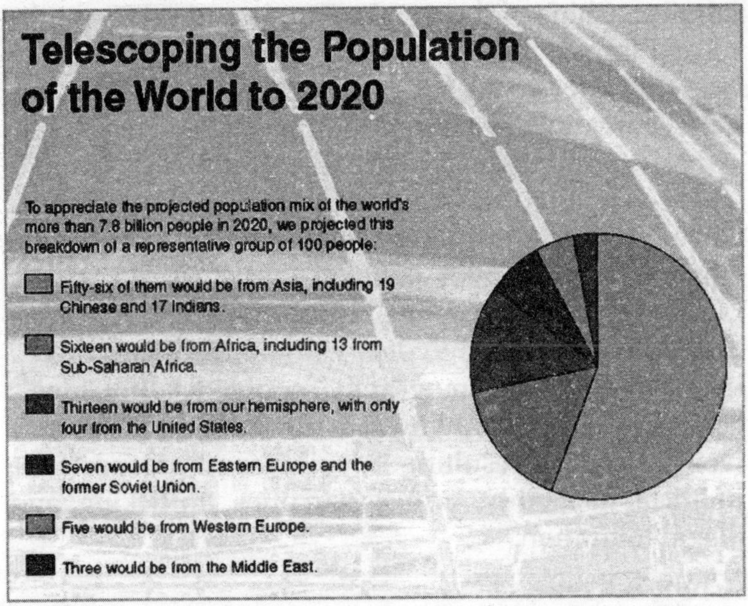

At the same time, other changes are likely to shape the new landscape. These include the possible economic rise of other states—such as Brazil, South Africa, Indonesia and even Russia—which may reinforce the growing role of China and India even though by themselves these other countries would have more limited geopolitical impact. The study also brought out the possibility of a stronger, more united Europe and a more internationally activist Japan, although Europe, Japan and Russia will be hard pressed to deal with aging populations.

China: The year 2020 is likely to witness China as an economic and military giant ready to flex its muscles. China will continue to strengthen its military through developing and acquiring modern weapons, including advanced fighter aircraft, sophisticated submarines and increasing numbers of ballistic missiles. China will overtake Russia and others as the second largest defence spender after the United States over the next two decades and will be, by any measure, a first-rate military power. On the flip side, economic setbacks and crises of confidence could slow China's emergence as a full-scale great power. The Chinese Government failure to satisfy popular needs for job creation could trigger political unrest. Faced with a rapidly aging society beginning in the 2020s, China may be hard pressed to deal with all the issues linked to such serious demographic problems. If China's economy takes a downward turn, regional security would weaken, resulting in heightened prospects for political instability, crime, narcotics trafficking and illegal migration.

China's Rise

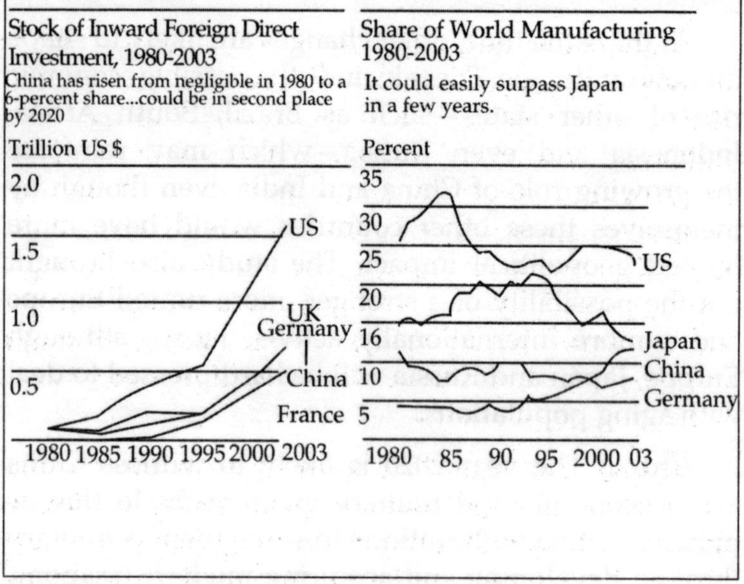

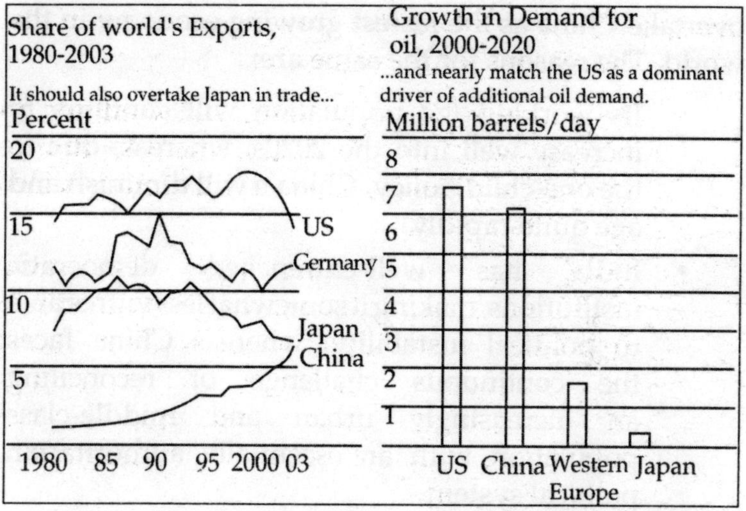

India: Like China, India is also likely to become a economic and military giant by the year 2020. India will seek to bolster regional cooperation both for strategic reasons and because of its desire to increase its leverage with the West, including in such organizations as the World Trade Organization (WTO). As India's economy grows, governments in Southeast Asia—Malaysia, Singapore, Thailand and other countries—may move closer to India to help build a potential geopolitical counterweight to China. At the same time, India will seek to strengthen its ties with countries in the region without excluding China. **Just like China, India may stumble and experience political and economic volatility with pressure on resources—land, water and energy supplies—intensifying as it modernizes.**

India lags economically behind China, according to most measures such as overall GDP, amount of foreign investment and per capita income. In recent years, India's growth rate has lagged China's by about 20%. Nevertheless, some experts believe that India might overtake China as the fastest growing economy in the world. The reasons for the same are:

- Its working-age population will continue to increase well into the 2020s, whereas, due to the one-child policy, China's will diminish and age quite rapidly.
- India has well-entrenched democratic institutions, making it somewhat less vulnerable to political instability, whereas China faces the continuous challenge of reconciling an increasingly urban and middle-class population with an essentially authoritarian political system.
- India possesses working capital markets and world-class firms in some important high-tech sectors, which China has yet to achieve.

India would be hard-pressed to accelerate economic growth rates to levels above those reached by China in the past decade. But China's ability to sustain its current pace is probably more at risk than is India's; should China's growth slow by several percentage points, India could emerge as the world's fastest-growing economy as we head towards 2020.

South Asia

Afghanistan is likely to remain an under developed state and in spite of a central government, will be influenced by tribal interactions and conflict. There is likely to be growing pressure on the central authorities to come down heavily on growing of opium and drug trade. However, opium will continue to remain the major cash crop of the region in foreseeable future.

Pakistan is likely to witness radical Islamisation, unemployment, slow growth and under-development. The situation is likely to become grim in case the political establishment is unable to implement good governance and rule of the land. The country will continue to be a significant transit area for Afghan drugs. In the absence of employment opportunities and legal means for political expression, conditions will be ripe for disaffection, growing radicalism, and possible recruitment of youths into terrorist groups.

Nepal will continue to an agricultural society with political instability which will hamper foreign investment and tourism. It has considerable scope for exploiting its potential in hydropower, with an estimated 42,000 MW of feasible capacity.

Bhutan will continue to be closely aligned with India through strong cultural and trade ties. Model education, social and environmental programmes which are currently underway will greatly enhance the social and economic outlook of the country in coming years.

Bangladesh is likely to witness severe effects of global warming including floods and rapid rise in mean sea level. Growing population coupled with poverty and unemployment will place enormous strain of the nation and could result in widespread migration of population into neighbouring India.

Sri Lanka will cash on an atmosphere of peace and tranquillity and make rapid strides in tourism and industry. It is likely to play a dominant role in protecting the sea lanes of communications passing through the Indian Ocean region.

European Union

The EU is likely to expand and add new East European nations to its fold. By most measures—market size, single currency, highly skilled work force, stable democratic governments, unified trade bloc and GDP—an enlarged Europe will have the ability to increase its weight on the international scene. Defence spending by individual European countries, including the UK, France and Germany is likely to fall further behind China and other countries over the next 15 years. Collectively these countries will outspend all others except the US and possibly China.[3] While its military forces have little capacity for power projection, Europe's strength may be in providing, through its commitment to multilateralism, a model of global and regional governance to the rising powers, particularly if they are searching for a "Western" alternative to strong reliance on the United States.

Aging populations and shrinking work forces in most countries will have an important impact on the continent, creating a serious but not insurmountable economic and political challenge. Europe's total fertility rate is about 1.4—well below the 2.1 replacement level. Over the next 15 years, West European economies will need to find several million workers to fill positions vacated by retiring workers.

An Expanding European Union

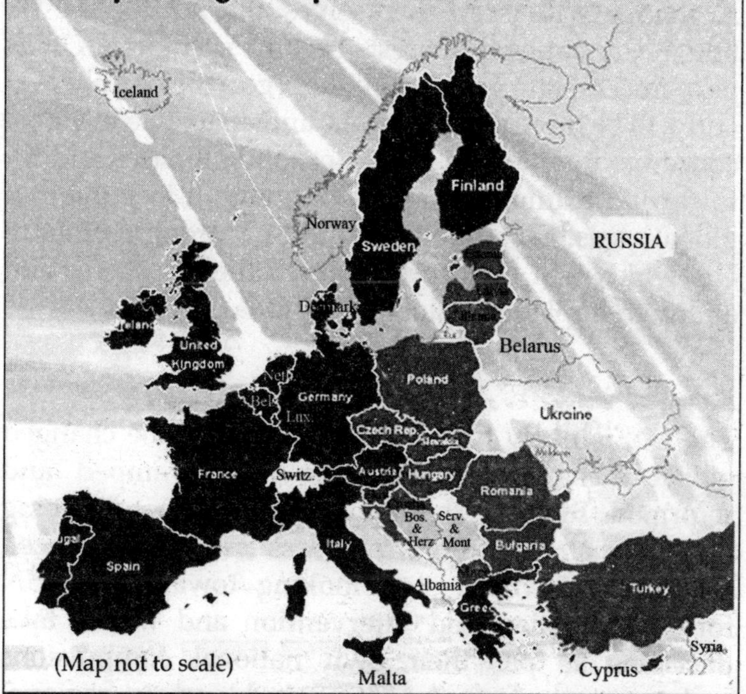

Current	European Union (EU) 15	EU 25	EU 30	China	Russia	US
Population (million)	380	458	527	1,299	144	293
GDP (billion US $)	11,000	11,637	12,091	6,449	1,287	10,980
Area (1,000 m²)	1,212	1,493	1,789	3,646	6,488	3,659

US

The US would continue to be the only super power in 2020 due to its military might and science and technology edge. However, continuous engagements in Iraq and Afghanistan-Pakistan would have a serious impact on its economic, military and diplomatic strength. US would continue to play the role of Big Brother in a complex geopolitical scenario, but individual countries like China, India, Brazil and Argentina will assert themselves and not toe the US line where national interests become surmount. On its part, the US state policy will undergo a major upheaval and will be more reconciliatory and amenable to global concerns. It will form new pacts and alliances and try to carry maximum nations along with it in pursuit of global goals. EU will turn out to be a strong partner to US, which will further strengthen the US power and ability to implement global decisions.

UN

The UN is likely to lose its relevance in the changed global scenario in case it is not revamped and reformed. By 2020, the likelihood of UN undergoing major transformations is very less and it is visualized that nations would stop looking towards the UN for reconciliation and intervention and would take decisions as per their own national compulsions and national strength. This would create regional imbalances, instability and unrest.

Economy

A nation's economy would be a major pillar of it's national strength. The US NIC report "Mapping the Global Future" predicts "We see globalization—growing inter-connectedness reflected in the expanded flows of information, technology, capital, goods, services, and people throughout the world—as an overarching "mega-trend", a force so ubiquitous that it will substantially shape all the other major trends in the world of 2020."[4] It further predicts that the world economy is likely to continue growing impressively:

by 2020, it is projected to be about 80% larger than it was in 2000, and average per capita income will be roughly 50% higher. By having the fastest-growing consumer markets, more firms becoming world-class multinationals and greater Science and Technology stature, Asia looks set to displace Western countries as the focus for international economic dynamism—provided Asia's rapid economic growth continues.

More firms will become global and those operating in the global arena will be more diverse, both in size and origin, more Asian and less Western in orientation. Such corporations, encompassing the current, large multinationals, will be increasingly outside the control of any one state and will be key agents of change in dispersing technology widely, further integrating the world economy and promoting economic progress in the developing world.

Certain key trends likely to be witnessed in the economic field by 2020 are:

- Rising Asia will continue to reshape globalization, giving it less of a "Made in the USA" character and more of an Asian look and feel.
- In terms of capital flows, rising Asia will accumulate large currency reserves or collectively three-quarters of global reserves—but the percentage held in dollars will fall.
- As governments devote more resources to basic research and development, rising Asia will continue to attract applied technology from around the world, including cutting-edge

technology, which should boost their high performance sectors.

- Increased labour force participation in the global economy, especially by China, India and Indonesia, will have enormous effects, possibly spurring internal and regional migrations.
- China and India because of their rising economic clout will seek more participation in International forums and decision making bodies.
- Competitive pressures will force major companies in the developed countries to outsource work in spite of having unemployment in their countries.
- In India, both the number of middle earners and their income levels are likely to rise rapidly, but their incomes will continue to be substantially below averages in the US and other rich countries even by 2020.

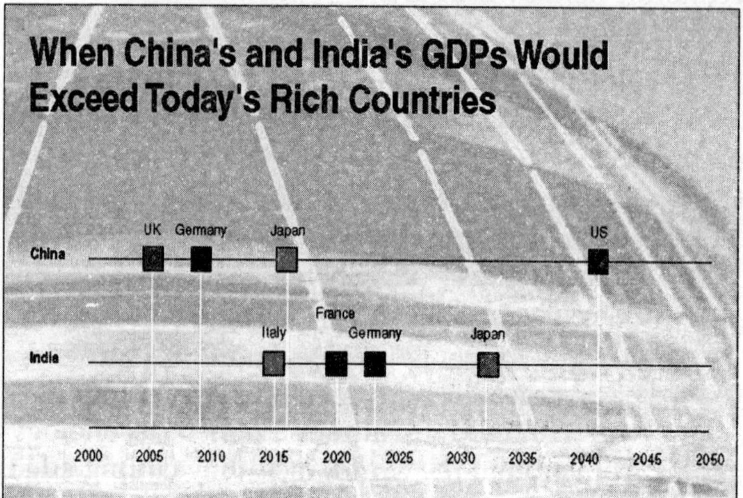

Source: Goldman Sachs, *Global Economics Paper No. 99*, October 2003.

Science and Technology (S&T)

Science and Technology (S&T) will be an important constituent of a nation's national power in 2020. New technology applications will foster dramatic improvements in human knowledge and individual well-being. Moreover, future technology trends will be marked not only by accelerating advancements in individual technologies but also by a force-multiplying convergence of the technologies—information, biological, materials and nano—that have the potential to revolutionize all dimensions of life. Materials enabled with nanotechnology's sensors and facilitated by information technology will produce myriad devices that will enhance health and alter business practices and models. Such materials will provide new knowledge about environment, improve security and reduce privacy. Such interactions of these technology trends—coupled with agile manufacturing methods and equipment as well as energy, water and transportation technologies—will help China's and India's prospects for joining the "First World."[5] The universalization of the Internet, both as a mass media and means of inter-personal communication, will help educate, connect, mobilize and empower those traditionally excluded.

Nations also will face serious challenges in oversight, control and prohibition of sensitive technologies. With the same technology, such as sensors, computing, communication and materials, increasingly being developed for a range of applications in both everyday, commercial settings and in critical military applications the monitoring and control of the export of technological components will become more difficult. Moreover, joint ventures, globalized markets and the growing proportion of private sector capital in basic R&D will undermine nation-state efforts to keep tabs on sensitive technologies.

Over the next 15 years, a growing range of actors, including terrorists, may acquire and develop capabilities to conduct both physical and cyber attacks against nodes of the world's information infrastructure, including the Internet, telecommunications networks, and computer systems that control critical industrial processes such as electricity grids, refineries and flood control mechanisms. A key cyber battlefield of the future will be the information on computer systems themselves, which is far more valuable and vulnerable than physical systems. New technologies on the horizon provide capabilities for accessing data, either through wireless intercept, intrusion into Internet-connected systems, or through direct access by insiders.

Global Energy Situation

An expanding global economy will increase demand for many raw materials, such as oil. Total energy consumed probably will rise by about 50% in the next two decades compared to a 34% expansion from 1980-2000, with a greater share provided by petroleum. Most experts assess that with substantial investment in new capacity, overall energy supplies will be sufficient to meet global demands. But on the supply side, many of the areas—the Caspian Sea, Venezuela and West Africa—that are being counted on to provide increased output involve substantial political or economic risk. Traditional suppliers in the Middle East are also increasingly unstable. **Thus sharper demand-driven**

competition for resources, perhaps accompanied by a major disruption of oil supplies, is among the key uncertainties. China, India, and other developing countries growing energy needs suggest a growing preoccupation with energy, shaping their foreign policies.[6]

Experts believe China will need to boost its energy consumption by about 150% and India will need to nearly double its consumption by 2020 to maintain a steady rate of economic growth. Renewable energy sources such as hydrogen, solar, and wind energy probably will account for only about 8% of the energy supply in 2020. While Russia, China and India all plan expansions of their nuclear power sector, nuclear power probably will decline globally in absolute terms in the next decade.

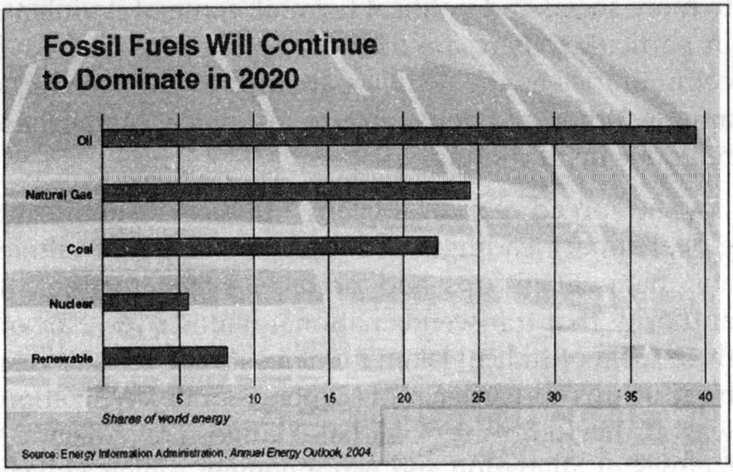

Terrorism and Islamic Fundamentalism

Part of the pressure on governance will come from new forms of identity politics centred on religious convictions and ethnic affiliation. Over the next

15 years, religious identity is likely to become an increasingly important factor in how people define themselves. The trend toward identity politics is linked to increased mobility, growing diversity of hostile groups within states, and the diffusion of modern communications technologies.[7] Trends seem to point toward growing numbers of converts and a deepening religious commitment by many religious adherents. Many religious adherents – whether Hindu nationalists, Christian evangelicals in Latin America, Jewish fundamentalists in Israel, or Muslim radicals – are becoming "activists". They have a worldview that advocates change of society, a tendency toward making sharp Manichaean distinctions between good and evil and a religious belief system that connects local conflicts to a larger struggle. At the same time, the desire by activist groups to change society often leads to more social and political turmoil, some of it violent. In particular, there are likely to be frictions in mixed communities as the activists attempt to gain converts among other religious groups or older established religious institutions.

The spread of radical Islam will have a significant global impact leading to 2020, rallying disparate ethnic and national groups and perhaps even creating an authority that transcends national boundaries. Part of the appeal of radical Islam involves its call for a return by Muslims to earlier roots when Islamic civilization was at the forefront of global change. The collective feelings of alienation and estrangement which radical Islam draws upon are unlikely to dissipate until the Muslim world again appears to be more fully integrated into the world economy. Radical Islam will continue to appeal to many Muslim migrants who are attracted to

Key Areas of Radical Islamic Activities Since 1992

(Map not to scale)

cope with superior strength. Asymmetric warfare can be used either in a war between states/coalitions or in a struggle between states and non-state actors. The weaker side, when fighting for core issues on which there is national consensus, may possess superior political will to achieve victory; and a preparedness to go for the long haul, if necessary to fight for decades. By contrast, an enemy engaged in a war of choice is likely to find it difficult to sustain political unity and the will to engage in a protracted struggle if battlefield success does not quickly lead to peace on his terms.[9]

References

1. Rajpal Budania, "The Emerging International Security System:

   Threats, Challenges and Opportunities for India"', Strategic Analysis, Vol. 27, No. 1, Jan-Mar 2003.
2. US National Intelligence report 2020, " Mapping the Global Future", p. 47.
3. Strategic Trends, Joint Doctrine and Concepts Centre, March 2003.
4. US National Intelligence report 2020, p. 10.
5. Ibid, p. 34.
6. Ibid, p. 12.
7. Ibid, p. 79.
8. CJ Dick, "The Future Of Conflict: Looking Out To 2020", Conflict Studies Research Centre, UK, p. 17.
9. Ibid, p. 25.

Chapter 5

Suggested Higher Decision-Making Structure

The present higher defence control structure of India is more or less of World War II vintage. At that point in time, national security was more or less synonymous with territorial integrity. The past two decades have witnessed a global explosion of information technology and enabling services. Internet and mobile telephony can be justifiably called the real game-changers in the global context in the past two decades. The resultant interconnect of people and organisations and the speed of passage of information has necessitated the requirement of speedy and accurate decisions in a complex environment with a great degree of uncertainty and complexity. Thus, it is imperative that speedy reforms be undertaken in the existing higher decision-making structure of India.

Areas of Improvement: India's Higher Defence Organisation

Inter-Service Jointness Inspite of a number of measures undertaken to increase inter-service cooperation and jointness, there still remains a lot which needs to be done. The following aspects merit attention:

- **Separate Commands for Each Service:** There are separate service commands with different geographical boundaries which lead a particular Air Force or Naval Command giving support to more than one Command of the Army. Also, it is felt that having one integrated Joint Command for a particular geographical area with elements of all the three services will reduce infrastructural requirements and lead to better decision making and jointness.
- **No Concept of Integrated Theatre Commands:** Assets of a particular service say Air Force or Navy are not placed under a Joint Theatre Commander for operational control. This, at times leads to lack of support and a classic example of an employee having two masters.
- **No Common Inventory of Similar Requirement of Arms/Equipment:** A number of weapons and equipment like small arms, communication sets, engineer plant equipment, light vehicles like trucks and jeeps/gypsies are used by all the three services but there is no commonality of these equipment leading to large inventory, separate tendering and lack of jointness. There is a requirement to have commonality of these weapons and equipment so that not only is the inventory reduced but

also common training can be imparted to all ranks of the three services.

- **Separate Training of Similar Trade Personnel:** Training of personnel of similar trade like drivers, cooks, operators, mechanics, fitters, masons, draughtsman etc. is done separately for each service. These personnel can be trained in common tri service institutions resulting in savings to the exchequer and a standard pool of common skill set across the services.

Lack of Coordination Amongst Various Intelligence Agencies: In spite of having a plethora of intelligence agencies, actionable intelligence is at times lacking, primarily due to time delays during intelligence sharing and hierarchical structure of the various agencies.

Void of a 24x7 Emergency Control Room: Barring the Police Control Rooms, we do not have a 24x7 Emergency control room at the centre to track the happenings across the country and directing and controlling operations which have a bearing on our national security. These could range from anti Naxal operations to our response to disasters to economic and cyber offences apart from full-fledged conventional wars.

Lack of a Fully Integrated Ministry of Defence: In spite of our best efforts, we do not have a fully integrated Ministry of Defence. There is a requirement of a fully enmeshed Ministry of Defence with all the three service headquarters. There is a requirement of 50% staffing in the ministry and the services headquarters of service and civilian officers. Also, the mix should range from the junior level to mid level to senior level officers.

Certain officers from the Ministry of Defence should also proceed on deputation to Command Headquarters and hard field stations to have a more intimate feel of the ground situation.

Lack of a National Security Audit Agency: Presently the Defence and Central Armed Police Forces are responsible for their internal audit on their operational readiness state. It is felt that there is a requirement of a National Security Audit Agency on the lines of Comptroller and Auditor General to carry out the national security audit of our Defence and Central Armed Police Forces.

A Unwieldy National Security Council: The present structure of the National Security Council is too top heavy and unwieldy. That is one of the reasons that there have hardly been any meetings of the National Security Council. This leads to lack of strategic leadership and vision and a poor decision-making as well as execution structure.

Lack of Time Bound Execution of National Security Policies/Directives: The national security strategic policies/directives require a coordinated and time bound effort on the part of the Defence/ Central Armed Police Forces, intelligence agencies and various other centre/state agencies. There is lack of monitoring and coordination within the various agencies resulting in inordinate delays, cost over runs and lack of accountability.

Void of Chief of Defence Staff (CDS): In spite of recommendations given by the Kargil Review Committee and the Group of Ministers, we still do not have consensus on a Chief of Defence Staff. This void of a CDS is resulting in lack of inter-service jointness, a service specific procurement policy, inter-service rivalry and no single point advice to the cabinet from the services point of view.

Organisational Changes at Defence Services Level

The following changes are recommended to be carried out at the services HQ level:

- **Formulation of Integrated Theatre Commands:** Rather than having different commands for Army, Navy and Air Force, it is suggested that we have integrated theatre commands namely Northern, Eastern, Western, Southern, South Western, Central, Andaman and Nicobar and Strategic Forces Command. The services be allowed to have their own training commands. The integrated theatre commander will have resources of all the three services under operational command. The service chiefs will be responsible for training and logistics of their own service elements. This system is in practice in the US Defence Forces.
- **Creation of Chief of Defence Staff (CDS):** The post of CDS be created at the earliest. The CDS will be senior to all the three service chiefs and will directly allocate resources to the Integrated Theatre Commands. He will be a four star general and appointed in rotation from all the three services. The CDS will offer a single point advice to the government.
- **Joint Staffing at Theatre Command HQs, Service HQs and Ministry of Defence:** To increase jointmanship and coordination it is recommended that we have joint staffing of all

headquarters by officers of all the three services and Ministry of Defence.

- **Common Training Infrastructure:** There is a requirement to have common training infrastructure for common trades like drivers, operators, mechanics, fitters, draughtsman etc.
- **Common Inventory:** The Defence Procurement Agency to ensure that all the three services use common arms/equipment as far as possible e.g. radio sets, small arms, radars, engineering equipment etc.
- **Joint Civil Military Operational Centre:** There is a requirement to set-up a joint Civil Military Operational Centre at all Integrated Theatre Command headquarters.

Organisational Changes at Ministry of Defence

The following changes at the Ministry of Defence are suggested:

- **Joint Staffing:** The Ministry of Defence to have joint staffing of at least 50% officers from all the three services. Similarly, the civil servants from the ministry to undergo cross attachment with the service headquarters as well at the theatre headquarters level.
- **Initial Probation of Officers:** All civil servants selected to join the Ministry of Defence to have a initial probation period of one year with all the three services prior to joining the ministry.

Organisational Changes of Intelligence Set-up

The following changes are recommended:

- **Joint Intelligence Analysis Wing:** Setting up of a Joint Intelligence Analysis Wing under the

National Security Advisor is proposed. The Joint Intelligence Analysis Wing will have officers on deputation from all the central intelligence agencies viz RAW, CBI, IB and NIA. The wing will function round the clock and provide daily, weekly and monthly summaries to the National Security Advisor and the National Security Council.

- **Accountability:** The concerned intelligence agency to be held accountable in case it fails to provide actionable intelligence preceding a major national security crisis like the Mumbai attacks or the Kargil intrusion.

Joint Threat Assessment Centre (JTAC): The JTAC will be the nerve centre of the higher decision-making structure. The JTAC will directly function under the National Security Advisor (NSA) and will have members drawn in from all the three services, Paramilitary forces, intelligence agencies and important ministries. The JTAC will directly report to the NSA and will be an independent and autonomous body. The JTAC will be responsible for the following:

- Provide Secretarial support to the NSC.
- Man the JTAC Operations room round the clock. Towards this end, the JTAC will have secure communications with the Operations room of the three services, National Disaster Management Agency and the Joint Intelligence Analysis Wing.
- Provide daily, weekly and monthly Threat Assessment Briefs to the NSA.
- Provide the Operational Support during natural calamity and external aggression.

National Security Audit Agency (NSAA): This is a new agency which is proposed to be formed on the lines of the Comptroller and Auditor General. The NSAA will be a fully independent and autonomous body under the National Security Advisor (NSA). To start with, the agency will comprise of officers on deputation from the armed forces, Central Armed Police Forces, intelligence agencies, key ministries and academicians dealing with national security. The role and responsibilities of the NSAA are as under:

- Be responsible to carry out a yearly audit of the capabilities and operational preparedness levels of our three services.
- The NSAA will be responsible to bring to the notice of the NSA the drawbacks in the operational preparedness levels as well as gaps in our national security infrastructure which need to be filled on priority.
- The NSAA will also be responsible to audit the capabilities of our Central Armed Police Forces.
- The NSAA will audit the functioning and output of various intelligence agencies.
- The NSAA will prepare a comprehensive document bringing out the national security achievements and challenges with regards to all facets of national security viz external, internal and border security.
- Carry out audit of our Research and Development Agencies.

In order to implement its job, the NSAA will be suitably empowered and would be provided unhindered access to all the HQs and units of all the

Services, agencies and branches dealing with national security.

Cabinet Committee on Security: No Change in the organizational structure of CCS is proposed.

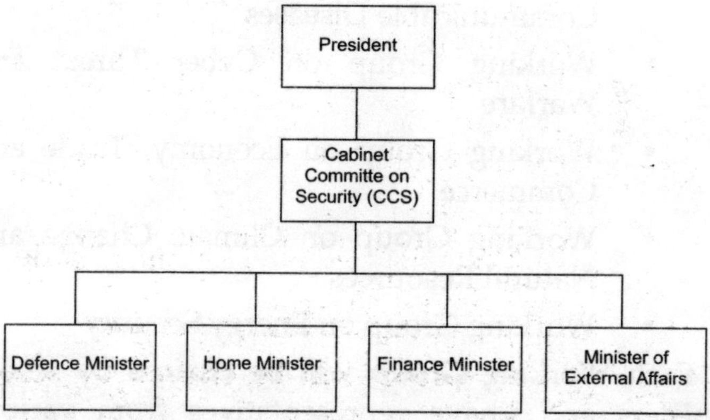

Organisational Changes in the National Security Council

As brought out earlier, the National Security Council is chaired by the PM and consists of the Strategic Policy Group, the National Security Advisory Board (NSAB) and the National Security Advisor. The secretarial support to the National Security Council is provided by the Joint Intelligence Committee. The following changes in the structure of the NSC are recommended:

- **Strategic Policy Group:** The Strategic Policy Group in its present stage is very unwieldy and consists of very high ranking officials which have operational as well as ceremonial roles. Hence, it is a matter of no surprise that the SPG has hardly got an opportunity to formally meet. It is therefore recommended that the Strategic Policy Group be replaced with the following working groups:

- Working Group on External Defence
- Working Group on Internal Security
- National Disaster Management Agency
- Working Group on Public Health and Communicable Diseases
- Working Group on Cyber Threat and Warfare
- Working Group on Economy, Trade and Commerce
- Working Group on Climate Change and Natural Resources
- Working Group on Energy Security

Each Working Group will be chaired by senior ministers and have representatives from various services, Paramilitary forces, intelligence agencies and ministries. The working groups will meet minimum twice a year at six monthly interval. Each of these working groups will function at three levels namely the Strategic Planning Group, Operational Planning Group and the Tactical Planning Group levels.

Strategic Planning Group (SPG): This group will consist of secretaries of concerned ministries and Heads of Services/Central Armed Police Forces/intelligence agencies. The SPG shall meet minimum once in three months and will shape the contours of the nation's national security infrastructure.

Operational Planning Group (OPG): Operational Planning Group will consist of middle rung officers of the ministries and organizations forming part of the particular working group. The main purpose of the OPG would be to brief the concerned strategic planning group of the actions undertaken/progress made on the policy guidelines/decisions taken by them, prepare briefs as well as discuss hurdles and road blocks encountered during the execution stage. It will be the principle inter-ministry/department coordination committee and will also supervise the functioning of the Tactical Planning Group. The operational Planning group will meet minimum once a month.

Tactical Planning Group (TPG): The Tactical Planning Group is the work-horse of all the working groups. It will work full time and meet daily. The TPG will consist of the middle/lower rung officers of the various ministries/departments and will be intimately associated with the Operational and Strategic Planning Group. The TPG will be responsible for the implementation of the policies of the Strategic and Operational Planning Group.

- **National Security Advisory Board (NSAB):** No change in the organizational structure of NSAB is proposed.
- **National Security Advisor (NSA):** The following organizations will function under the NSA:
  - Joint Threat Assessment Centre (JTAC)
  - Joint Intelligence Analysis Wing (JIAW)
  - National Security Audit Agency (NSAA)

The diagrammatic structure of the proposed National Security Council is as follows.

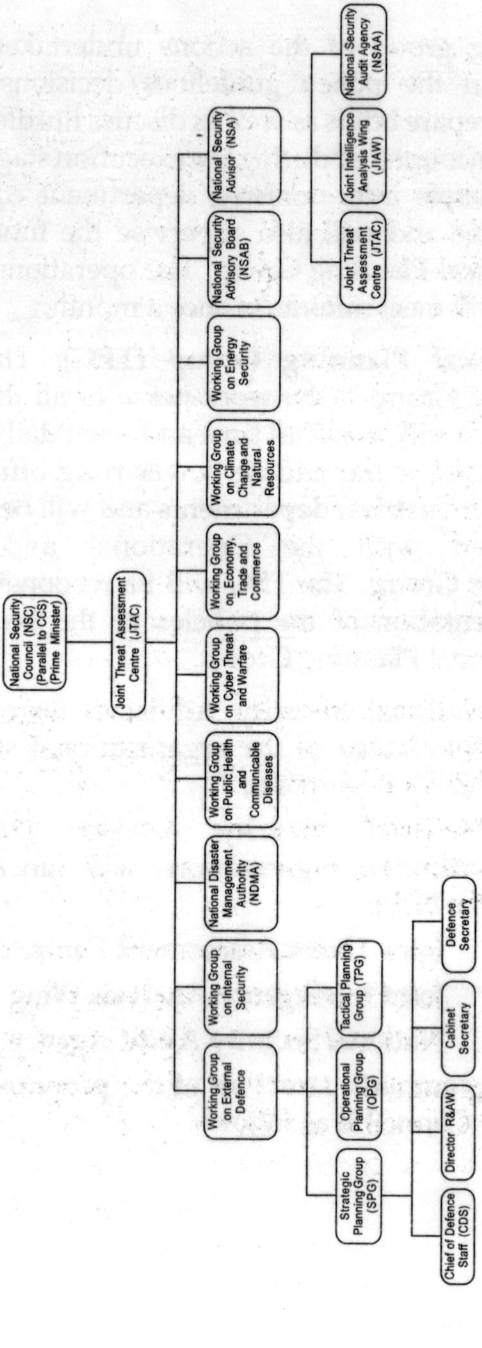
National Security Council (NSC) (Parallel to CCS) (Prime Minister)
Joint Threat Assessment Centre (JTAC)
Working Group on External Defence
Working Group on Internal Security
National Disaster Management Authority (NDMA)
Working Group on Public Health and Communicable Diseases
Working Group on Cyber Threat and Warfare
Working Group on Economy, Trade and Commerce
Working Group on Climate Change and Natural Resources
Working Group on Energy Security
National Security Advisory Board (NSAB)
National Security Advisor (NSA)
Joint Threat Assessment Centre (JTAC)
Joint Intelligence Analysis Wing (JIAW)
National Security Audit Agency (NSAA)
Strategic Planning Group (SPG)
Operational Planning Group (OPG)
Tactical Planning Group (TPG)
Chief of Defence Staff (CDS)
Director R&AW
Cabinet Secretary
Defence Secretary

Strategic Force Command: The Strategic Force Command would be responsible for the operational preparedness, safety and readiness of the country's strategic weapons including their delivery means. Due to the nature of their tasks, the organization, command and control set-up and force structuring of the Strategic Force Command would be kept as a national secret. The Commander, Strategic Force Command would report directly to the Cabinet Committee on Security and would not fall under the purview of either the National Security Audit Agency (NSAA) or the Chief of Defence Staff.

Frequently Asked Questions

Q1. What is Information Warfare? Describe its constituents.

Information warfare may be defined as all actions undertaken by an individual, group, organization or nation to prevent an adversary in using his information, information based networks or processes and at the same time ensuring full use of own information, information based networks and processes. There are seven forms of information warfare namely Command and Control Warfare (C2W), Intelligence Based Warfare (IBW), Electronic Warfare (EW), Psychological Warfare (PSW), hacker warfare, Economic Information Warfare (EIW) and cyber warfare.Details of the same are as under :-

(a) **Command & Control Warfare (C2W).** It is the military strategy that implements Information Warfare on the battle field and integrates physical destruction. Its objective is to decapitate the enemy's Command structure from its body of command forces.

(b) **Intelligence Based Warfare (IBW).** It occours when intelligence is fed directly into operations (notably targeting and battle damage assessment) rather than used as an input for overall command and control. The aim is to reduce the time lag between the sensor and the shooter in order to enable faster, lethal and accurate response to a situation.

(c) **Electronic Warfare.** It attempts to degrade transfer of information over the electromagnetic spectrum.

(d) **Psychological Warfare.** It encompasses the use of information against the human mind. It has four parts namely operations against the national will, operations against opposing commanders, operations against troops and cultural conflict.

(e) **Hacker Warfare.** These are attacks on computer networks and systems through the exploitation of knowable holes in the systems security structure. The common hacking tools used are viruses, logic bombs, Trojans, sniffers, worms and bots.

(f) **Economic Information Warfare (EIW).** It can take place in two forms i.e. Information Blockade and Information Imperialism. In Information Blockade nations would strangle each others access to external data (a major catastrophe in a fully networked and enmeshed global scenario) which would cripple the economies of those nations. Information Imperialism implies that an information superior nation would acquire and reinforce highly complex and specialist knowledge intensive skills against which other nations, especially those with low wage work force, cannot easily compete.

(g) **Cyber Warfare.** It is a broad category comprising of information terrorism and semantic attacks. Information terrorism is a subset of computer hacking aimed not at disrupting systems but at exploiting them to attack individuals. Similarly, a system under semantic attack will be perceived as operating correctly but will generate answers at variance with reality.

Q2. How is climate change affecting our national security?

Climate change is a significant and lasting change in the statistical distribution of weather patterns over periods ranging from decades to millions of years. It may be a change in average weather conditions, or in the distribution of weather around the average conditions (i.e., more or fewer extreme weather events). Climate change is caused by factors such as biotic processes, variations in solar radiation received by Earth, plate tectonics, and volcanic eruptions. Certain human activities have also been identified as significant causes of recent climate change, often referred to as "global warming".

The sharp variations in the global climate in the last 50 years have been attributed to human activity due to increasing atmospheric concentration of green house gases, deforestation and increasing atmospheric concentration of aerosols.

Global warming is defined as an increase in the average temperature of the Earth's atmosphere, especially a sustained increase great enough to cause changes in the global climate. Records show that the past 25 years have been the warmest time of the past 5 centuries. The global warming has resulted in the warming of the oceans, rising of the sea levels, melting of glaciers, and diminished snow cover in the Northern Hemisphere.

The recent catastrophic climatic events like the massive floods in Pakistan and India, the Hurricane Katrina in the United States, the prolonged droughts in Australia, China, Pakistan, India and Texas, are all the results of increased temperatures due to global warming. During the 21st century, climatic disasters occurred five times as frequently and killed or affected seventy times as many people.

There has been a particularly alarming effect of global warming on the climate of India. India is already a disaster prone area, with the statistics of 27 out of 35 states being disaster prone, with most disasters being water related. The process of global warming has led to an increase in the frequency and intensity of these climatic disasters. According to surveys, in the year 2007-2008, India ranked the third highest in the world regarding the number of significant disasters, with 18 such events in one year, resulting in the death of 1103 people due to these catastrophes. Global warming is also posing as a mammoth threat to the foods security situation in India with recurring and severe droughts and ravaging floods engulfing the arable land. Rising Temperatures on the Tibetan Plateau are causing the melting of the Himalayan glaciers, reducing the water flow in the rivers Ganges, Brahmaputra, Yamuna, and other major rivers, on which the livelihoods of hundreds of thousands of farmers depend.

According to the Indira Gandhi Institute of Development Research, if the process of global warming continues to increase, resulting climatic disasters would cause a decrease in India's GDP to decline by about 9%, with a decrease by 40% of the production of the major crops. One of the direct impact of climate change is growing food insecurity, especially in countries like India where farmers are predominantly dependant on stable climate and monsoons for food production. However, industrial food production is one of the leading causes of increased emission of green house gases due to large scale deforestation for growing crop and pasture, CO2 emissions during crop production and transportation, methane being produced by livestock and Nitrous Oxide by chemical fertilizers. The fact that food production is both damaged by Green House Gases and a source of Green House Gases makes it doubly important that climate change and food security be given top priority. This is not the case at present. Both aspects are being practically ignored, all attention being given to fossil fuel CO2 emissions. If we don't control food production emissions our food production today will damage food production in a few decades from today. So our food security depends on changing food production practices today to control emissions - as well as stopping fossil fuel CO2 emissions.

Q3. Define Human Rights. How does violation to these constitute a threat to our national security?

"We hold these truths to be self-evident, that all men are created equal, that they are endowed by their Creator with certain unalienable Rights, that among these are Life, Liberty and the pursuit of Happiness."

—United States Declaration of Independence, 1776

Human rights are those fundamental rights to which a person is inherently entitled simply because she or he is a human being. Human rights can be classified and organized in a number of different ways, at an international level the most common categorisation of human rights has been to split them into civil and political rights and economic, social and cultural rights.

Civil and political rights are enshrined in articles 3 to 21 of the Universal Declaration of Human Rights (UDHR) and in the International Covenant on Civil and Political Rights (ICCPR). Economic, social and cultural rights are enshrined in articles 22 to 28 of the Universal Declaration of Human Rights (UDHR) and in the International Covenant on Economic, Social and Cultural Rights (ICESCR). Some of the substantive human rights are right to life, freedom from torture, freedom from slavery, right to a free trial, freedom of speech, freedom of thought, conscience and religion and freedom of movement.

Violations of individual or collective human rights are a serious crime which needs to be dwelt with seriously. However, when states resort to collective human right like genocide and use of inappropriate force then it is the collective responsibility of the international community to deal with the concerned state and restore human rights of the effected population.

Ensuring protection of human rights of its citizen within and outside the country is one of the primary tasks of a nation state.

Q4. What do you understand by Revolution in Military Affairs (RMA)?

Militaries, the world over have benefitted if they had a superiority edge over their adversaries. Invention of gun powder and cannon ensured the demise of hand to hand combat as the predominant method of war fighting and acted as a force multiplier by providing victory to a relatively numerically inferior but technologically superior army.

With the advent of information age, there has been unprecedented improvement and innovation in military technology especially in the fields of stealth, intelligence, surveillance and reconnaissance, command, control, communication and information processing and precision strikes. This evolution in weapons, equipment and information technology has resulted in a paradigm shift in the manner in which wars are conducted as well as in the military doctrine and organizations. Collectively, this phenomena where in a technologically advanced military can have unprecedented advantage over its adversary is referred to as Revolution in Military Affairs or RMA.

RMA results in a shorter Observe Orient Decide Act (OODA) loop, real time passage of information from sensor to shooter, precision strike, complete battle field transparency, seamless connectivity and enhanced night vision capabilities.

Q5. What do we understand by the term "Weaponisation of Space"?

"The United States considers space capabilities—including the ground and space segments and supporting links—vital to its national interests. Consistent with this policy, the United States will: preserve its rights, capabilities, and freedom of action in space; dissuade or deter others from either impeding those rights or developing capabilities intended to do so; take those actions necessary to protect its space capabilities; respond to interference; and deny, if necessary, adversaries the use of space capabilities hostile to U.S. national interests;

The United States will oppose the development of new legal regimes or other restrictions that seek to prohibit or limit U.S. access to or use of space. Proposed arms control agreements or restrictions must not impair the rights of the United States to conduct research, development, testing, and operations or other activities in space for U.S. national interests;"

> National Space Policy, Office of Science and Technology Policy, Executive Office of the US President, October 6, 2006

The United Nations (U.N.) Outer Space Treaty provides the basic framework on international space law, saying that space should be reserved for peaceful uses. It came into effect in October 1967. The treaty includes the following principles:

(a) The exploration and use of outer space shall be carried out for the benefit and in the interests of all countries and shall be the province of all mankind;

(b) Outer space shall be free for exploration and use by all States;

(c) Outer space is not subject to national appropriation by claim of sovereignty, by means of use or occupation, or by any other means;

(d) States shall not place nuclear weapons or other weapons of mass destruction in orbit or on celestial bodies or station them in outer space in any other manner;

(e) The Moon and other celestial bodies shall be used exclusively for peaceful purposes;

(f) Astronauts shall be regarded as the envoys of mankind;

(g) States shall be responsible for national space activities whether carried out by governmental or non-governmental activities;

(h) States shall be liable for damage caused by their space objects; and

(i) States shall avoid harmful contamination of space and celestial bodies.

However, most of the world's powerful nations including USA and China have ambitious plans to utilize space as the fourth frontier and a dominant military arena.

Weaponisation of Space would involve firstly development of technology and capability to place weapons in space, destroy or degrade an adversary's space assets and prevent access to space.

Anti Satellite Weapons. These consist of missiles launched from air or sea based platforms to destroy the adversary's satellites orbiting the earth at various altitudes. In 2007, China demonstrated a land based anti satellite weapon system by destroying one of their own weather satellite. The US likewise shot down a crippled spy satellite in 2008 with a sea based missile system. The debris generated by this action will orbit the Earth and can be hazardous to own manned space missions and satellites.

Directed Energy Weapon System. These weapons use high energy LASERS, microwave and particle beams to physically destroy or degrade the electronic components and systems of an adversary's space assets.

High Altitude Electromagnetic Pulse (EMP) Generators. These weapons will generate a high energy burst of electromagnetic radiation to produce current and voltage surges anywhere on Earth immediately crippling all electronic devices in the area. These EMP bursts are generally associated with nuclear explosions but scientists have now produced non – nuclear EMP devices.

Space Based Space Surveillance (SBSS) System. This is a US Air Force planned constellation of satellites supported by ground based stations to detect and track hostile space based assets of the adversary. The first "Pathfinder" satellite of the SBSS was launched on 25 September 2010.

Space Based Positioning and Timing Systems. Global Navigation Satellite System (GNSS) allow specialized radio receivers on Earth to determine their 3 D space coordinates and time. The space coordinates are utilized by a number of military systems including homing and tracking systems on missiles. Countries which possess their own GNSS have an unprecedented advantage over the countries which do not possess these systems. The countries with existing systems include GPS of USA, GLONASS of Russia and Beidou of China.

Q6. How many Combatant Commands are there in the United States Defense Forces? Describe their Areas of Operations and Chain of Command.

A Unified Combatant Command (UCC) is a United States Department of Defense Command that is composed of forces from at least two Military Departments and has a broad and continuing mission. These Commands are established to provide effective command and control of U.S. military forces, regardless of branch of service, in peace and war. They are organized either on a geographical basis (known as "Area of Responsibility", AOR) or on a functional basis. UCCs are "joint" commands with specific badges denoting their affiliation.

Each Unified Command is led by a Combatant Commander (CCDR), who is a four star general or admiral. The operational chain of command flows from the President to the CCDR through the Secretary of Defence.

Presently, US has nine Combatant Commands of which six are based on Areas of Responsibilities and three on functional basis. The various Combatant Commands are :-

(a) United States Africa Command. Raised on 02 Oct 2007 and stationed at Kelley Barracks, Stuttgart, Germany.

(b) United States Central Command. Raised on 01 Jan 1983 and stationed at Mac Dill Air Force Base, Florida.

(c) United States European Command. Raised on 15 Mar 1947 and stationed at Patch Barracks, Stuttgart, Germany.

(d) United States Northern Command. Raised on 01 Oct 2002 and stationed at Peterson Air Force Base, Colorado.

(e) United States Pacific Command. Raised on 01 Jan 1947 and stationed at Camp HM Smith, Hawai.

(f) United States Southern Command. Raised on 06 Jun 1963 and stationed at Miami, Florida.

(g) United States Special Operations Command. Raised on 16 Apr 1987 and stationed at Mac Dill Air Force Base, Florida.

(h) United States Strategic Command. Raised on 01 Jun 1992 and stationed at Offutt Air Force Base, Nebraska.

(i) United States Transportation Command. Raised on 01 Jul 1987 and stationed at Scott Air Force Base, Illinois.

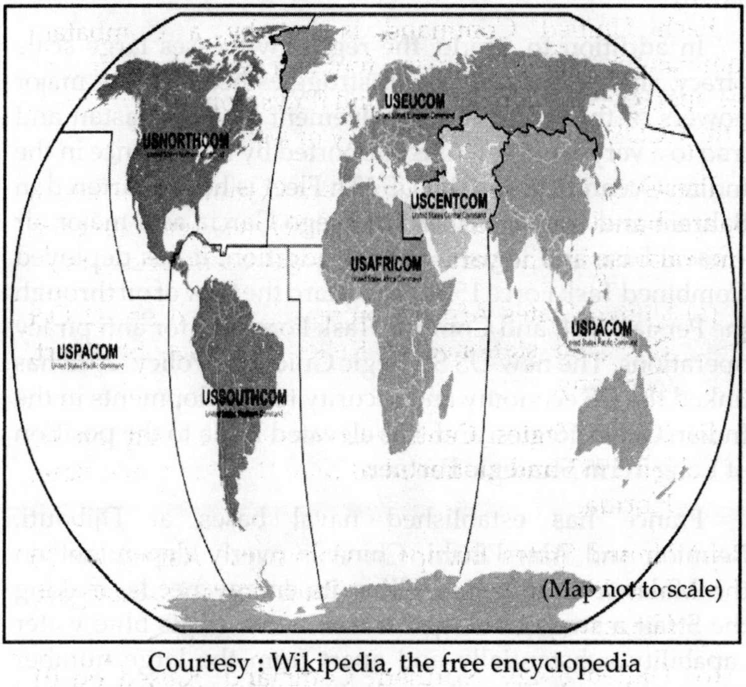

Courtesy : Wikipedia, the free encyclopedia

Q7. Elaborate on the strategic importance of Indian Ocean Region.

The Indian Ocean is the third largest water body in the world and contains some of the most vital and strategic important sea lanes. It has 36 states around its littoral belt. In addition there are 11 landlocked states like Nepal and Afghanistan who are heavily dependant on the ocean.

More than 80% of the world's sea borne trade in oil transits through the Indian Ocean choke points, with 40 % passing through the Strait of Hormuz (Between the Gulf of Oman and the Persian Gulf, Iran and UAE, Oman), 35 % through the Strait of Malacca (Between Malaysia and Sumatra island of Indonesia) and 8 % through the Bab el Mandab Strait (Located between Yemen on the Arabian Peninsula, Djibouti and Eritrea, north of Somalia, in the Horn of Africa, and connecting the Red Sea to the Gulf of Aden).

In addition to trade, the region witnesses large scale piracy, smuggling and power struggles between the major powers of the world. US involvement in Afghanistan and Iraq to a very large extent is supported by its presence in the Indian Ocean Region. The US 5Th Fleet is headquartered in Bahrain and uses the island of Diego Garcia as a major air – naval base and logistic hub. In addition, it has deployed Combined Task Force 152 to safeguard the flow of oil through the Persian Gulf and Combine Task Force 150 for anti piracy operations. The new US Strategic Guidance Policy 2012 has linked the US economy and security to developments in the Indian Ocean Region and has elevated India to the position of Long Term Strategic Partner.

France has established naval bases at Djibouti, Reunion and Abu Dhabi. China is overly dependant on the Malacca Strait for fulfilling its energy needs, making the Strait a strategic target. It has increased its blue water capability substantially and apart from the large number of ocean based assets has a large number of shore based establishments including listening posts and logistic hubs. China has also pursued an aggressive soft power diplomacy policy by providing large loans with generous repayment options, investing in major infrastructure projects to include building of roads, ports, power plants, dams etc. and has secured considerable goodwill in the region.

The UN Food and Agriculture Organisation have admitted that 75 % of fishing resources in South – Western Indian Ocean Region have been fished to their limit by countries outside the region. This is drastically impacting the majority of poor countries of the region who depend on primitive and non mechanical methods of fishing to earn a livelihood and feed their families.

Courtesy : Wikipedia, the free encyclopedia

Q8. Bring out the major recommendations of Group of Ministers (GoM) on National Security

The Group of Ministers (GOM) was set up in April 2000 to review the national security system in its entirety and in particular to consider the recommendations of the Kargil Review Committee and formulate specific proposals for implementation. The GOM under the Chairmanship of Shri LK Advani also included the Defence Minister, External Affairs Minister and Finance Minister.

The GOM set up four Task Forces, one each on Intelligence Apparatus, Internal Security, Border Management and Management of Defence. These task forces were multi disciplinary in nature and made up of domain experts. The GOM held a total of 27 meetings. The Cabinet Committee on Security (CCS) considered the GOM report on 11th May, 2001 and decided that the recommendation in respect of the institution of the Chief of Defence Staff (CDS) be considered later, after Government is able to consult various political parties. It accepted all other recommendations contained in the GOM report.

The recommendations given by the GOM were :-

(a) The establishment of an Intelligence Coordination Group (ICG) and Technology Coordination Group (TCG), working in close tandem with National Technical Facility Organisation (NTFO).

(b) The appointment of a Chief of Defence Staff, with administrative control over India's Strategic Forces Command, as the focal point for military advice to the Government.

(c) Preparation of a holistic 15-20 year Defence Perspective Plan, subject to rigorous inter and infra service prioritisation backed by a Defence Procurement Board.

(d) Progressive decentralisation of decision making and delegation of powers to Service Headquarters, with them becoming Integrated Headquarters of the Ministry of Defence rather than "Attached Offices".

(e) Revamping of Defence Information relations together with quick-responding media cells in field formations.

(f) The establishment of a National Defence University.

(g) The Economic Intelligence Council is to be refurbished and given a wider mandate.

(h) The State Police and Central para-military forces are to be modernised with a new orientation being given to weapons, equipment and training.

(i) Border Management is to be re-fashioned on a one-border-one-force principle.

(j) The Coast Guard is to be strengthened and a specialised Marine Police to be raised in all coastal States and island territories.

(k) Sanctity of Indian airspace is to be safeguarded inter-alia through procurement of additional low level transportable radars, integrated air command and control systems, integration of national radar resources, revamp of airspace management of coastal and island territories etc.

(l) The national security structures will be backed up by a rejuvenated Civil Defence Organisation, village and ward defence committees and a revamped criminal justice system backed by laws and regulations appropriate to emerging circumstances.

(m) The programme to institute a multi-purpose National Identity Card is to be vigorously pursued, commencing with all border districts.

(n) Modalities are to be evolved for involving youth in national service in conformity with the spirit of Article 51 A(d) of the Constitution.

Q9. What is Network Centric Warfare?

Network Centric Warfare (NCW) is a military doctrine that seeks to translate Information Technology enabled information superiority into a strategic military advantage achieved through networking of forces and processes across the entire spectrum of forces.

There are four tenets of NCW :-

(a) A robustly networked force improves information sharing.

(b) Information sharing enhances quality of information and shared situational awareness.

(c) Shared situational awareness enables the following :-

- (i) Collaboration and self synchronization.
- (ii) Enhanced sustainability of force.
- (iii) Effectiveness of command, control and decision making.

(d) This results in increased mission effectiveness and acts as a force multiplier giving an unprecedented advantage to the force.

Index